'A pricker o...
and deceptions...
Fascinating' Susan F...

'The book of the career of th...
happens, she says, when a nosy chil...
perfect job' *Independent on Sunday*

'Terrific . . . Lynn Barber can take an over-interviewed, not-terribly-interesting celebrity and write 5,000 words about them that are so clever, bold and funny you want to read to the very end' *Financial Times*

'Candid and extremely entertaining . . . Packed with anecdotes illuminating both her own and her interviewees' lives . . . I read this in a sitting, unable to stop smiling' *Woman & Home*

'Full of observational insights and salty asides. She really is the best in the business . . . A hugely enjoyable read' *Evening Standard*

'This memoir is laugh-out-loud funny and, at some points, almost unbelievable – but Lynn Barber is her usual honest self . . . I found Barber's sincerity and warmth completely captivating. ****' *Stylist*

'A frank and funny memoir . . . A razor-sharp insight into the lives of the mega-famous, the world of journalism and Lynn's own extraordinary life' *Hello!*

A NOTE ON THE AUTHOR

LYNN BARBER is an award-winning British journalist. Several collections of her interviews have been anthologised. She read English Literature at Oxford, worked for *Penthouse* magazine for seven years, then for the *Sunday Express*, *Independent on Sunday*, *Vanity Fair*, *Observer* and *Sunday Times*. Her books include two collections of interviews, *Mostly Men* and *Demon Barber*, as well as two sex manuals and a study of Victorian naturalists. Her memoir, *An Education*, was made into an award-winning film starring Carey Mulligan and Rosamund Pike. She lives in north London.

LYNN BARBER

A Curious Career

BLOOMSBURY

LONDON · NEW DELHI · NEW YORK · SYDNEY

Bloomsbury Paperbacks
An imprint of Bloomsbury Publishing Plc

50 Bedford Square   1385 Broadway
London   New York
WC1B 3DP   NY 10018
UK   USA

www.bloomsbury.com

BLOOMSBURY and the Diana logo are trademarks of Bloomsbury Publishing Plc

First published in Great Britain 2014
This paperback edition published 2015

British Library Cataloguing-in-Publication Data
A catalogue record for this book is available from the British Library.

ISBN: HB: 978-1-4088-3719-1
PB: 978-1-4088-3721-4
ePub: 978-1-4088-3720-7

2 4 6 8 10 9 7 5 3 1

Typeset by Hewer Text UK Ltd, Edinburgh
Printed and bound in Great Britain by CPI Group (UK) Ltd, Croydon CR0 4YY

To find out more about our authors and books visit www.bloomsbury.com.
Here you will find extracts, author interviews, details of forthcoming
events and the option to sign up for our newsletters.

For Rosie and Theo

CHAPTER ONE

The Value of Nosiness

Growing up in Twickenham in the 1950s I could never have said my ambition is to be a celebrity interviewer because that career didn't even exist then. Of course newspapers sometimes ran interviews with famous people, generally politicians, but always in a news context: What are your plans, Mr Prime Minister? The idea of asking famous people incredibly nosy questions about their personal lives hadn't yet been invented. I was fortunate to come along at just the right time.

My ambition as a child was to be some sort of writer, probably a novelist. But my *hobby* as a child was being nosy. I really was (but why put it in the past tense? I still am) exceptionally nosy. I want to understand other people, I want to know what they think, what they do when I'm not there, how they interact, especially with their families, and how they got to be how they are.

I used to believe that everyone must secretly be as nosy as me but that some of them were better at hiding it. I now know that's not true. I've come to realise over the years that many – perhaps the majority – are not actually all that interested in others. Presumably they would *say* they are – if you gave them a tick-box questionnaire they would say, 'Oh yes, I'm interested in other people,' just as they would say, 'Oh yes,

I have a great sense of humour,' but in reality quite a lot of them are lying. They don't suffer from my compelling nosiness. They don't really wonder how on earth A came to marry B, or what they get up to in bed. They don't wonder if C had an unhappy childhood, or why D has fallen out with his sister. Basically, they prefer talking about themselves to listening. Their loss, I think. But perhaps I spend too much time wondering about other people. If it wasn't that I make my living from it, it would, I suppose, be quite unhealthy.

The reasons for my nosiness are not far to seek. I was an only child, and a very isolated one, in that my parents didn't have any family or friends, or any who ever came to the house. Of course I met girls my own age at school, but there was a whole world of other people – boys primarily, but also older children, younger children, other parents – I was eternally curious about. I wanted to see how other families interacted because I dimly (but accurately) felt there was something not quite right about mine.

Partly it was a class thing. My parents were both from working-class backgrounds but had risen through education into the middle class – Mum a teacher, Dad a Civil Servant – but I think they still felt a bit precarious, like first-generation immigrants. Dad never attempted to disguise his working-class roots and managed to retain his strong Lancashire accent all his life; he would reprimand my mother if he felt she was 'putting on airs'. And yet he was the one who insisted that I go to a private school, Lady Eleanor Holles, five miles away when I could easily have gone to Twickenham County Grammar just across the road.

I went to Lady Eleanor Holles on a scholarship but most of the pupils were fee-paying and from affluent families. They lived in detached houses in Surrey, they talked about their fathers' new cars, some of them even had ponies. They regularly invited me to their homes but I rarely if ever invited them to mine. Actually, *qua* house, it was perfectly acceptable, a biggish three-bedroom Edwardian job with a conservatory and long back garden, but it was No. 52 in a terrace of identical houses, not up a drive like most of my schoolfriends'. And of course it contained my father. He would sit in his armchair and shout orders intended to carry round the house – 'Don't make a noise,' 'Turn that light off,' 'Where's my tea?' – which visitors found alarming. I was so used to his shouting I barely noticed it, but I could see it was scary for other people.

My schoolfriends, I felt, came from 'proper' families. They had brothers and sisters and fathers (whom they actually called 'Father') who did something in the City, and drove a car and played golf (mine played bridge – he was a Civil Service champion) and mothers who stayed at home and cooked. Mum didn't cook, ever – we lived on tinned food and Birds Eye Roast Beef Dinners For One – whereas she did, embarrassingly, work from home by giving elocution lessons. Unusually for the 1950s, my parents did equal shares of housework, which was yet another reason for not bringing friends home – they might find Dad doing the ironing while singing his 'marching songs' – 'Hitler Has Only Got One Ball', or 'She'll Be Coming Round The Mountain'. We were not the sort of family you came across in Enid Blyton – or indeed *anywhere* as far as I could see.

So I was naturally curious about how proper families operated and persistently asked questions – questions that other people often found peculiar. 'Does your brother know that you have periods?' was a big obsession in my teens, because I couldn't imagine the embarrassment of sharing a bathroom with a *boy* – in those days, periods meant sanitary towels and a special bin to put them in. 'Does your mother kiss your father when he comes home from work?' was another perennial, and – a real giveaway, this – 'Does your father ever shout at your mother?'

I think my schoolfriends found all my questioning weird, but they also acknowledged its usefulness: I was always the one deputed to ask Virginia if she'd snogged the Hampton Grammar boy who took her to the cinema last night. My friends wouldn't ask because they considered it uncool to seem interested, but it was OK to send me because everyone knew that I was nosy. They also thought I had an almost magical ability to get secrets out of people, perhaps by some form of hypnosis. But actually I found then and still find now that if you bounce up to someone and say, 'Everyone is dying to know whether you went out with so-and-so and what he was like,' they're usually so flattered by your interest, they'll tell you. Of course it's a *bit* more difficult with people in the public eye but the principle holds good – the more interested you are, or seem to be, the more willing they are to divulge. And so eventually this became my career: asking questions that other people wanted to know the answers to but were too embarrassed to ask.

But before that, on the cusp of adulthood, I learned the damaging effect of *not* asking questions. At sixteen, I was picked up by a much older man in a red sports car who became my boyfriend for the next two years. But, because I was trying desperately to seem more sophisticated than I was,

I failed to deploy my usual nosiness. So I never asked him his age, or where he lived, or how he made his money (by working for Peter Rachman and passing dud cheques was the answer – he went to prison later). Above all, I didn't ask, because it never occurred to me, whether he was married. He meanwhile was busily persuading my parents to let me marry him instead of going to Oxford. He actually convinced them – they were on his side – but luckily I found out about his existing wife (and children) in the nick of time and went to Oxford while he went to prison. But that episode, which later became the film *An Education*, taught me about the value of nosiness and the dangers of not asking questions.

I feel the fun began at Oxford. I never took much interest in my Eng Lit course but I *loved* the social life. In those days – the 1960s – there were seven male undergraduates to every female and if you were reasonably pretty, as I was, you got asked out constantly, to punting picnics, cocktail parties, dinners at the Elizabeth. I don't think I ate a meal in college the whole time I was there – I was royally wined and dined and of course in those days girls were never expected to pay for anything. In my second year, I was given a wonderful new invention, the Pill, and celebrated with a bout of wild promiscuity. But then, in my very last term, I fell in love. His name was David Cardiff and I *knew* from the moment I met him that he was the man I must marry.

Not for one minute at Oxford did I ever think about what I could do for a career. While other undergraduates were filling out application forms for banks, or Unilever, or the Civil Service, I was hanging round coffee bars hoping to run into David. Finding the right husband was *far* more important than finding the right job, I felt (and still feel). So I left Oxford with absolutely no career prospects. My parents had made me do a shorthand-typing course before I went to university and I'd done a lot of office temping in the vacations, so I knew I could earn money doing that. But of course it was deadly boring so I had to think of something else. While I was still at school, I'd written stories and articles for the children's page of my local newspaper, the *Richmond and Twickenham Times*, and – this is the important bit – *been paid for them*. So I knew that I could potentially earn money by writing. How, though? Journalism seemed the easiest option but at that time newspapers were a closed shop, controlled by the NUJ, and you could only get into them via one of their traineeship schemes which meant working on a regional paper. But how could I work on a regional paper when I had to be in London to pursue David?

The only hope was magazines, though many of those were already unionised too. But, while at Oxford, I'd done an interview for *Cherwell* (the student newspaper) with Bob Guccione, an American entrepreneur who was then launching a new men's magazine called *Penthouse*, in imitation of *Playboy*. We got on well and he said at the end, 'If you ever want a job, honey, come to me.' I laughed gaily, thinking things would never come to *that* pass, but after several months of writing to other magazines and being told they had no vacancies, I wrote to Bob at *Penthouse* and, sure enough, was offered a job as editorial assistant. It paid £16 a week which was not bad for those days – enough to buy a new outfit every week at Biba. I didn't have to pay rent because I was David's girlfriend by this time and we spent all our time staying with his friends – luckily, having been to Eton, he had plenty of rich ones.

My duties at *Penthouse* included, among other things, interviewing people with unusual sexual tastes for an everlasting series called 'Parameters of Sexuality'. These people were definitely *not* celebs – they were foot fetishists, voyeurs, transvestites, dominatrices, men who liked wearing nappies – you could say that, as an interviewer, I started at the bottom.

But actually it was all good training – learning to use a tape recorder, learning to ask open-ended questions designed to draw people out, learning not to seem shocked or disapproving of the answers, learning to press for more detail and not be content with generalities. It was easy in one way, in that my interviewees were volunteers who were only too eager to talk for hours (anonymously of course) so I never suffered from the celebrity interviewer's twin bugbears of limited time and limited personal revelation – my problem always was getting away. If, nowadays, people are sometimes surprised that a nice respectable lady like me can ask such embarrassing questions, that's only because they don't know about my seven-year apprenticeship at *Penthouse*.

It was *Penthouse*, too, that gave me my first big celebrity interview, with Salvador Dali, in 1969 when I was twenty-five. Bob Guccione growled at me one day, 'You speak French, don't you, honey?' I made some non-committal noise. 'Get over to Paris and interview Salvador Dali – he's at the Hotel Meurice.' At the Meurice I was met by a short dapper Irishman who introduced himself as Captain Moore, Dali's secretary, and took me along miles of corridors to Dali's suite. He advised me to address Dali as 'Maître' which I found quite easy when I met him – he was so tall, so old, so grand, I almost wanted to genuflect. Guccione had told me to ask Dali his views on sex (I hardly needed telling) and I struck gold with my very first question, about his habits. 'Ha-beets! Ha! First masturbation. *Le mast-urb-ation*, you know? Zee painters are always zee big masturbators – nevaire make love, only watch, and *some-times* masturbation! Zat is one good habit. Zee other is *foot*.' What? '*Foot!* Zee heating.' He gestured to his mouth and I realised he meant food, eating. 'I lika very much the crayfish and ortolan because I lika very much food with faces. No food I eat without faces. I like to look at everything and then eata the everything. When I see people with limousine, with rings on hand, I want to eata everything.'

Dali enjoyed being interviewed so much that he kept shouting 'More! More!' so I asked about his daily life in Cadaques. 'My day the most regular possible. Wake at nine, in bed working till eleven. Lunch. Go for leetel swim, making no movement [he demonstrated floating on his back]. After a siesta of twenty-five minutes, then working, then nude girls come for me to watch – no touch – then some drawing. At six o'clock make peepee and at eight many pederasts arrive, because Dali like zee androgyne people. No lika de sex – one man, one woman – like better confusion, you know?' He also told me, 'Every big artist, every important people – Michelangelo, Leonardo, Napoleon – is impotent and this is good. Because if you work too well with your sex you never produce nozzing. Only childs. But for artist, le libido and le sexual instincts sublimate in the artistic creation.'

As I was bowling questions at Dali, and he was shouting his answers in increasingly fractured English, I noticed other people gathering in the room, listening in. Then a very hirsute man backed through the double doors dragging a lifesize human dummy and Dali spent some time laying it out on the floor with a cushion under its head, a stringless lute behind, and a map of Brest and one of La Rochelle under each shoulder, while the retinue clustered round admiring it. Nobody, including me I'm ashamed to say, asked what it was meant to represent, but we all oohed and ahed at this work of genius. But then Dali's wife Gala walked in, and the retinue fell silent and gradually drifted away. Everyone, it seemed, was terrified of Gala. She looked very chic in a red-and-white Chanel suit and I would have guessed her age at fifty but Captain Moore told me later she was eleven or twelve years older than Dali, so probably seventy-six.

The Captain explained that Dali and Gala always lunched alone but he would take me to lunch with his fiancée, Katherine, and – an unexpected bonus – Dali's ocelot. Luckily the other people in the Meurice dining room seemed quite happy to have an ocelot in their midst. After lunch, the Captain and Katherine took me back to their flat and suggested I might like to join them for a threesome (one of the hazards of working for *Penthouse* was that people were *always* asking me to join them for a threesome) but I gave my usual answer that it was 'not the right time' so they showed me their fascinating collection of Dali artefacts instead.

Dali had said he would see me again for five o'clock tea but when I went back to his suite a Japanese journalist was already battering him with questions and soon a troupe of actors called the Living Theatre led by Julian Beck walked in. They fell on the drinks trolley and all the pyramids of bonbons scattered round the room. One of the girls took a bite of one of them and spat it out – 'Jeez-us, what the hell is this?' I told her it was a marron glacé, a crystallised chestnut, and she put her face very close to mine and hissed, 'Listen, baby, don't try to get smart. I seen chestnuts, and they don't come all slimy like that godawful crap.' Retreating from her, I thought I'd introduce myself to Madame Dali because she was sitting alone, so I said I was a journalist from London and she screamed, 'I never give interviews. Never. Never. Never,' while simultaneously patting the sofa to indicate I should sit beside her. 'Are there always so many people here?' I asked, trying to make conversation. 'Listen. They are very interesting people. Why should Dali see you and not them – you think you are better?' Agh. I could see why people avoided Gala.

By this time I was desperately worried about my flight – I was supposed to fly back the same night – but Dali said we would talk again in the morning. I explained that I had nowhere to stay in Paris, so he told the Captain to find me a room at the Meurice, which he did. So then I interviewed Dali the next day, and the next, and the next, and in the evenings I went to parties in his suite, and gobbled my way through all the pyramids of marrons glacés dotted round the room. I was present one morning when the Captain brought in a French couple carrying two enormous packets of thick paper and I watched Dali signing each sheet 'Dali 69'. When I asked what he was doing, he said, 'I am manufacturing money' – apparently he signed them and the publisher later added a doodle and sold them as Dali drawings. Eventually

Gala started giving me the evil eye and Dali said regretfully that he thought we had done enough interviewing. But he presented me with a wonderful gift – a conical hat made of wax flowers and butterflies that he had designed for Gala to wear to a fancy dress ball in the 1930s. When, years later, I lent it to a Dali exhibition in Stuttgart, they insured it for £15,000. So that was my first celebrity interview, which naturally made me want to do more.

I kept dropping hints to Guccione, so eventually he sent me to Ravello, Italy, to interview Gore Vidal. Alitalia lost my case on the way, so I arrived in a rumpled dress and terrible plastic shoes but again my subject was kind and said I must stay while Alitalia found my luggage. Vidal virtually interviewed himself, telling a well-honed string of anecdotes – but I noticed that, when the tape ran out in the middle of an anecdote, he stopped and waited while I turned the tape over – no point in wasting a good anecdote on a silly girl when it was intended for the world. He and his companion, Howard Austin, took me out to dinner (still in my plastic shoes) in Ravello that night, and got very loud and jolly on crème de menthe. I have never, before or since, seen anyone drink crème de menthe right through a meal. Rather to my regret, Alitalia returned my suitcase the next day so I had no further excuse to linger.

Soon afterwards, I left *Penthouse* and spent several years as a full-time mother. (There was no question of maternity leave in those days.) David and I were married in 1971 and had our first daughter, Rosie, in 1975 and our second, Theo, in 1978. We lived in Finsbury Park which was considered a dangerously rough area in those days, though I notice that nowadays it counts as 'desirable' and has been renamed Stroud Green. I did the usual rounds of mother-and-baby club, playgroup, nursery, and made some good friends. David was teaching media studies (a brand-new subject in those days) at the Regent Street Polytechnic, and I had some residual income from two sex books, *How to Improve Your Man in Bed* and *The Single Woman's Sex Book*, that I wrote while I was at *Penthouse*. During these playgroup years, I wrote a very different book, *The Heyday of Natural History*, on a subject that then interested me, Victorian popular naturalists. It got rapturous reviews when it was published in 1980 and gave me a sort of respectability but I look at it now and think: What a waste of time. I dedicated it to my mother, thinking it would make up for my sex books, but she only said she liked the illustrations! Weirdly, it is still in print in Japan and brings me an annual royalty cheque of £60 or £70.

Once both daughters were settled at school, I was desperate to get back into journalism. But it is hard – and I feel great sympathy for young women today – to apply for jobs when you have known nothing but playgroups for several years. I'd forgotten what office clothes even looked like. But by the happiest of happy chances my original boss at *Penthouse*, Harry Fieldhouse, who taught me to be a journalist in the first place, had moved to a newly launched colour supplement, the *Sunday Express Magazine*, and asked me if I'd like to do a series for it called 'Things I Wish I'd Known at 18'.

This was one of those 'back of the book' features, like the *Sunday Times'* 'Life in the Day', which entailed interviewing a celeb, and cobbling their answers together into a single long quote. It was a boringly narrow formula, but it did give me a very wide experience of dealing with celebs and getting over the inevitable beginner's problem of being star-struck. Finding celebs was easy in those days – you could often get their addresses, or even their phone numbers, from *Who's Who* – there was none of the nonsense of having to pre-negotiate everything with PRs. And I soon learned that actors who were stuck in long West End runs were *desperate* to be interviewed – after the first-night excitement died away, they often felt forgotten by the world.

In 1983 a new editor, Ron Hall, joined the *Sunday Express Magazine*, and promoted me to writing 'big' interviews – no longer back of the book, but proper 3,000-word profiles. My breakthrough came when he sent me to New York to interview my old boss, Bob Guccione. Up till then, I'd been writing all my profiles in the third person, as was the custom then, but I thought: I *have* to say I used to work for Guccione, it would be mad not to. So I wrote the piece in the first person and felt that at last I was writing without constraint. It was a really joyous, liberating moment, the point at which I found my writing voice.

I won my first British Press Award in 1986, and my second the next year, which reassured me that I was on the right track. Older, stuffier journalists lectured me about 'objectivity' and told me it was wrong to put myself in my articles, but, with two Press Awards under my belt, I was happy to ignore them. In 1990 the *Independent* launched a Sunday sibling, the *Independent on Sunday*, and hired me as their interviewer. It enabled me to write very long (5,000-word) interviews, which I preferred, and won me a couple more Press Awards. But I also acquired the nickname 'Demon Barber' which was a pain for a long time. It gave the impression that I *only* wrote hatchet jobs, which was unfair – I probably only wrote one or two a year, but they tended to be the ones that stuck in people's memories. And, for all the glittering company at the *Independent* (Ian Jack, Zoë Heller, Sebastian Faulks, Blake Morrison, Nick Cohen, Alexander Chancellor, Francis Wheen, Michael Fathers), I found it an unhappy ship, riven by internal feuds and institutional sexism. So I was glad to move on to *Vanity Fair*, and then the *Telegraph* and the *Observer*, before settling into my present home, the *Sunday Times*.

People sometimes ask why I'm *still* doing interviews as I approach my seventieth birthday, in a tone which suggests I could be doing something more respectable like – oh! – writing books. To me that's a bit like saying to a good cook, 'You don't *still* need to cook meals, do you, when you could afford to go to restaurants?' But why give up something you adore doing? Once in a while, when it's my third actor in a row, I might start grumbling, 'This is a waste of my time,' but basically that phone call from my editor – 'Do you want to interview Pete Doherty? Miranda Hart? Eddie Izzard?' – brings a little leap of excitement to my heart. Even when the name is someone I've never heard of (Lady Gaga, shockingly, but it WAS the very start of her career) my reaction is always to say yes, and then to do some frantic Googling later.

The only people I flatly refuse to interview are ones I know to be boring (usually because I've interviewed them before or met them socially) or ones I don't think are worth five pages of the readers' attention. I also have a block about doing what I think of as 'wives' (they could also be husbands, or lovers) who are only famous second-hand by virtue of their partner, and I deeply hate doing 'victims' or people with heart-breaking stories to tell. I want my subjects to have achieved *something* in their own right, even if it's the sort of something that broadsheet readers don't necessarily approve of. I once got a lot of flak for interviewing Kerry Katona – why were posh *Observer* readers supposed to be interested in her? Actually I thought her achievement – to survive a hideously chaotic upbringing and forge a career as a pop star, columnist, and all-round celeb – was pretty impressive, even heroic. I think we despise such people at our peril.

Being so nosy, and being a professional interviewer, makes it hard for me to be a guest at dinner parties. I have to keep reminding myself that it's not actually polite to ask, 'What happened to your last girlfriend?' Or (which I have been known to do), 'What happened to your face?' You have to waste time fishing around and even then you often come away without a proper answer. I find it frustrating, maddening – I can't actually do dinner parties. On the other hand, if I get stuck in and start asking all the nosy questions I want answered, people are sometimes a bit too flattered, a bit too thrilled. They are apt to phone me afterwards wanting to continue the conversation: 'When I was telling you about my last girlfriend . . .' And, worse, they expect me to remember everything they told me before whereas, without a tape recorder, the chances of my remembering anything at all are slim. The great thing about interviews is that you can have a very intense conversation, and then switch off your tape recorder, write the article, and forget about it. Celebs understand that. But it is harder in real life.

I have quite often been described as 'fearless' which makes me laugh. Just see me in a field full of cows, or in a lift that gets stuck between floors. Try taking me on the Tube. I am fearful of many things, including fish, but I am not on the whole fearful of asking people questions. After all, it is very unlikely that anyone would commit murder in an interview and I suppose I have the advantage, as a woman, that no one is likely to punch me.

But by fearless I think people mean I don't have the normal English fear of social embarrassment. I don't worry about making a fool of myself or seeming stupid. I've never felt any desire to be cool. And if a conversation takes a nasty turn, if I provoke someone into losing their temper or shouting at me, well it's all familiar stuff because I spent eighteen years in Twickenham being shouted at by my father. I think this is something that perhaps confuses people about me. I have a genteel accent and come over as (I think) a harmless middle-class woman. But actually, I'm not the pussycat I appear. I'm quite tough, as my interviewees sometimes find out.

When I started, I was often asked why I chose to interview stars, why didn't I interview 'real people'? The obvious answer is that readers are more interested in stars. But then, so am I. I admire them for their talent, but even more for the courage it takes to become a star, to leave the cosy camaraderie of the herd. And I'm always interested in what gave them the drive to do that. A few stars like to maintain that it all happened by accident (Michael Palin is the worst offender) but I don't think it *ever* happens by accident – there has to be some special talent and then, much rarer, there has to be the drive to keep on keeping on through all the discouraging years when nothing seems to be happening. There are no easy routes to stardom, despite the delusive propaganda of shows like *The X Factor*. Even someone like Susan Boyle had a long history of singing in talent shows before she made her big breakthrough. Nearly all comedians – Paul Merton, Michael McIntyre, Jack Dee, Eddie Izzard – plugged away for years on the club circuit before literally 'getting their act together' and being noticed. It's quite rare to meet a star who *hasn't* been on the dole at some time. But that's what's impressive: they would rather live in squats and survive on benefits, following their dream, than take a safe job.

I admire people who have taken risks – I always feel I've played far too safe myself. And I like it best if they've come a long way. My 'journey' has taken me all the way from Twickenham, west London, to Highgate, north London, my furthest detour being the three years I spent at Oxford. Contrast that with someone like Rudolf Nureyev – born in Ufa in a remote Soviet republic, the son of a minor Party functionary, got himself to Leningrad to star in the Kirov, went on tour with the Kirov abroad, heard in Paris that he was being sent back to the Soviet Union and decided on the spur of the moment, at the airport, to defect to the West. He had no time to say goodbye to his Kirov colleagues and friends; he would not see his mother again until the very end of her life. At that stage he barely spoke English or French – by the end he was fluent in at least five languages, was director of the Paris Opera Ballet, and a collector and connoisseur of antiques and paintings. He told me it seemed amazing to *him* when he tried to remember his boyhood in Ufa – so long ago, so far away, it felt like a different world.

Nureyev, like so many of my interviewees, educated himself as he went along, all through his life. He learned almost nothing at school, but when he wanted to learn ballet, he found a ballet teacher, when he wanted to learn French, he found a French teacher. This is something that has struck me time and again while interviewing people – that all their most valuable education happened outside school. An amazing proportion of them – possibly a third – say they were useless at school, often because of undiagnosed dyslexia. But also, perhaps, because they didn't take orders easily and didn't accept the goals their schools were pushing. They were the brave souls, the mavericks, the awkward squad, who said they wanted to do something different with their lives. I hugely admire them.

CHAPTER TWO

As Good As It Gets

My idea of a hellishly boring interviewee is one who is obviously nice, sane, polite, who chats pleasantly, is happy to answer your questions and clearly has nothing to hide. Where's the fun in that? Give me a monster every time – someone who throws tantrums, hurls insults, storms out, and generally creates mayhem. So welcome, Marianne Faithfull! This is probably the most enjoyable interview I've ever done. It won me my fifth Press Award. I came out of our encounter thinking: I can't *wait* to write this up. And when my editor rang the next day to ask how the interview went, instead of my usual laconic, 'Not bad,' I said firmly, 'It was *great*!'

From the *Observer*, 15 July 2001

Marianne Faithfull once said, 'I am a Fabulous Beast, and as such, I should only be glimpsed very rarely, through the forest, running away for dear life.' How wise she was. If I were ever asked to interview her again, I would turn into a Fabulous Beast myself and hightail it to the forest. I first glimpsed Her Fabulousness ages ago at a restaurant in Notting Hill, 192, where she was sitting all alone at lunchtime reading the papers. 192 was a very sociable sort of

19

table-hopping restaurant, so I thought there was something faintly sad about her solitude. But then a man joined her – it might even have been my future nemesis, François – and she simply handed him a slice of newspaper and carried on reading right through lunch. It was so devastatingly drop-dead cool that all the chattering at the other tables somehow died – we farmyard animals knew we were in the presence of a Fabulous Beast.

So when I heard she was coming to London (she lives in Dublin) to publicise the film *Intimacy*, I jumped at the chance to interview her. It all seemed quite straightforward: she would go to David Bailey's studio at 12.30 p.m. to have her photo taken – she likes David Bailey, they 'go back a long way', to the 1960s – and I would pick her up at 4 p.m. and interview her till 6 p.m. when a car would take her to the airport for her flight back to Dublin. My only worry (ha ha, in retrospect) was where I could take her between 4 p.m. and 6 p.m., because I thought that as a reformed junkie she wouldn't fancy a wine bar. Silly old me.

At 1 p.m., the publicist phones to say Marianne has not yet arrived at Bailey's – she was still in bed when they rang at 12.45 p.m. – so everything has been put back an hour. Fine, or fine-ish. I arrive at Bailey's studio eager-beaver at 5 p.m., and walk into an atmosphere you could cut with a knife. Marianne, trussed like a chicken in Vivienne Westwood with her boobs hanging out, ignores me, Bailey likewise; half a dozen assorted stylists, hairdressers, make-up people stand around looking tense. The PR is friendly but apologetic – she says the photographs will take at least another hour and I should push off and have coffee. A Frenchman who looks like

Woody Allen but without his suavity and charm introduces himself as François Ravard, Marianne's manager. I wait for some apology or explanation of why they are running two hours late – it never comes. Finally I say, 'You're running late?' 'Ah yes,' he says with a shrug. 'You know how it eez – it eez always the same.' Really? 'But don't worry,' he adds, 'we have dinner later.' Thanks a million, *mon frère* – I was supposed to be having dinner with friends. I push off to make calls cancelling my evening.

When I return to Bailey's, the atmosphere is even worse. No sign of Marianne – she has gone off to change – Bailey looks like thunder. Various sotto voce conversations are going on around me and I hear the ominous phrase from Bailey 'as long as it takes'. Time for my tantrum, I feel. Choosing my spot carefully, I stamp my feet like a flamenco dancer and address the studio at large. 'There is no point in taking photographs,' I warble, 'unless there is an article to stick them in. And there is no article unless I get my interview NOW.' The hair and make-up people stare blankly – so uncool! – but Bailey's assistant and the PR seem to get the point and agree that they will shoot one more pose and finish at 6.15 p.m. This news is relayed to Bailey with much fierce muttering and hostile staring at me. I decide to go outside and do some deep breathing.

When I get back, Bailey is at the camera; Marianne, in a black mac and fishnet tights, is sprawling with her legs wide apart, her black satin crotch glinting between her scrawny fifty-five-year-old thighs, doing sex-kitten moues at the camera. 'Oh please, stop!' I want to cry – this is sadism, this is misogyny, this is cruelty to grandmothers. I wonder if Bailey actually hates her – I wonder if this is her punishment for turning up late. I hear the agent and the Frenchman muttering behind me – 'They won't use this, they can't.' So why is Bailey shooting it then?

Suddenly, the session is over, and we – Marianne, the Frenchman, the PR and me – emerge into the street where a chauffeur-driven limousine has been waiting all this time. It is now 6.45 p.m. and Faithfull has still barely said hello. The PR says we can eat at the Italian restaurant at the end of the street. Marianne says she can't possibly walk, so we pile into the limousine to drive 50 yards to the corner. It is a sweet, friendly, family-run Italian restaurant that has no idea what hell awaits it. No sooner have we been ushered into a private room downstairs than Marianne is muttering, 'What do you have to do to get a drink around here?' Order it, seems the obvious answer, but that's too simple – François has to order it for her. Unfortunately – my huge mistake – I have let him and the PR eat downstairs with us, albeit at a separate table, and even more unfortunately I have placed Marianne against the wall, where she can see François over my shoulder. I could smack myself: what's the use of serving all these years in the interviewing trenches if I still make such elementary mistakes?

Suddenly, Marianne is shouting at François, 'Get it together!' and he is shouting back, 'What do you want, Marianne?' 'I don't know. What have they got?' she counters, drumming her feet under the table and moaning, 'I. Can. Hardly. Bear. It.' François keeps asking whether she wants wine or a cocktail. I'm thinking rat poison. Eventually she tells François a bottle of rosé. The waiter brings it with commendable speed and starts pouring two glasses. She snatches mine away – 'We don't need that. Where's the ice bucket?' The waiter goes away and comes back with an ice bucket. 'I'll have the veal escalope,' she tells him. He waits politely for my order. 'Veal! *Vitello!*' she snaps – she can't understand why he is still hanging around when he should be off escaloping veal. 'I'll have the same,' I say wearily.

I'm already fed up with her and we haven't even started. But at this point – a tad late, in my view – she suddenly flicks the switch marked 'Charm' and bathes me in its glow. 'Cheers!' she says. 'Sorry I yelled. A slight *crise* there. It's been a long day.' (Really? She was still in bed at one, it is now seven, hardly a full shift at the coalface.) But anyway, she is – finally – apologetic. And I in turn put on my thrilled-to-meet-you face and tell her that I deeply enjoyed her autobiography *Faithfull* (1994), which I did. It is a truly amazing story – a pop star at seventeen, a mother at eighteen, Mick Jagger's girlfriend at nineteen, reigning over Cheyne Walk – and yet by her thirties she was a heroin addict living on the street in Soho. Even if she didn't write a word of it (David Dalton was co-author), she deserves some credit just for living it. For a while she basks in my compliments and then switches off the charm and snaps, 'But I'm not going to talk about the book, I want to talk about the film.' Huh? Too late I realise my mistake with the placement – obviously there has been some signal from François.

So then she launches into her spiel about *Intimacy* – how she saw Patrice Chéreau, the director, in a Paris restaurant and rushed over to tell him she loved his film *La Reine Margot* and to ask, 'Can I be in your next film?' He said yes, and started writing a part for her that night. It is quite a small part, as a loopy bag lady, but Chéreau evidently convinced her it's the pivot of the film. Did she mind having to look so unglamorous? 'I did and I didn't. The first time I saw it, it was a shock. But I would jump off a cliff for Patrice. I don't know why, but I really fell in love with him and I want to work with him again. He's one of the reasons I'm doing this interview. I want the film to be a success – I want Patrice to go on making films in English so I can work with him again.'

Actually, I would have thought that Patrice Chéreau's career could survive without the services of a ratty old rock chick. But let that go – she is very good in the film, however briefly. She has always had the potential to be a good actress, but four years ago she told the *Radio Times*, 'I was never an actress. That's a waste of my time.' So is she an actress or isn't she? 'Well, you know I love acting, but I haven't ever made it my priority. Maybe that was a mistake. But I couldn't help it. Music really is my life. And nearly every film I've been in has been crap, except *Hamlet* [with Nicol Williamson], which is brilliant. And I've ended up very fond of *La Motocyclette* [*The Girl on a Motorcycle*] although it was a horrible experience to make. But honestly, the rest of the filmwork I've done has been ghastly. So I used to feel, till now, that I hadn't had the opportunity to be in really good films with really good directors. Because I could have been a really good actress – and I still could.'

Yet, judging from her book, she had endless opportunities to be a good actress, but invariably blew them away by turning up to work drugged to the eyeballs or not turning up at all. It might have been an obscure desire to punish her mother who had huge ambitions for her little princess. But also she was hell-bent on becoming a junkie from the moment she read *The Naked Lunch* – she wanted to be a junkie more than she wanted to succeed as an actress or to marry Mick Jagger. Jagger was surprisingly patient for a long time – he took the rap for her in the notorious drugs bust at Redlands when he claimed her pills were his. (Incidentally, she says about the drugs bust that, yes, she was naked under a fur rug – but it was a very large fur rug – and no, there was no Mars bar involved. But she hasn't eaten one since.)

She split with Jagger in 1970 and became a full-time heroin addict, living in squats and on the street. But she was lucky in that friends got her on an NHS drugs programme, which meant she could get her daily fix on prescription from the chemist. She had one of the highest dosages going – 25 jacks of heroin a day. It left her with poor circulation which is still evident in her angry-red, mottled arms.

It is a mystery what she lived on in the 1970s – she says it's a mystery to her, too. 'I don't know how I survived. There was a time after the 1960s, when I was – I call it depressed – where there was absolutely no income. But I managed somehow. My parents didn't have any money. I didn't sell my body. I don't know how I managed. Flying through life on charm, I suppose. But I never took unemployment, welfare, ever. I have a thing about it.' Scratch an old hippie, find a Thatcherite, as Julie Burchill always says. Faithfull was far too hoity-toity to do anything as common as signing on. She always made sure people knew her schoolteacher mother was a baroness (Austro-Hungarian, natch). There is a theory that Jagger only embarked on his social mountaineering to impress Faithfull, because she sneered at him for being middle class – of course he totally gazumped her within months. Anyway, she 'lived on her wits' and according to Chris Blackwell of Island Records was very good at touching people such as doormen for the odd fiver or tenner.

What drove her to drugs? 'I don't know that anything drove me. I didn't even like it that much either; I just think it was like a good anaesthetic.' But she says in her book that she always had an attraction to the 'Dionysian' life. 'And I still do!' she grins. 'I'm always going to be drawn to that sort of fantasy. Though nowadays I don't do anything about it.' Does she still take drugs? 'Occasionally. I'm not going to go into it. Obviously no heroin. And I don't at all trust all these new drugs; they're not a good idea. But you know I'm a very decadent person, I really am. Whether I'm on drugs or not, it doesn't change anything. I can see why I liked them, and I can't sort of put that down. It's just if you want to do anything else in your life, it doesn't really go.'

She had one failed detox in England in the early 1980s, and then went to Hazelden, the Minnesota clinic, in 1985 and cleaned up. She stayed completely clean, and went to NA meetings for five and a half years. She also moved to Ireland, to the remote and beautiful Shell Cottage on a country estate in County Wicklow, and lived very quietly, alone. She had friends three miles down the road, but she couldn't walk that far and couldn't drive. 'It felt very lonely, and I was there nine years, and it's a long time to be all on your own. But I'm very glad I did and it was really great for my spiritual life.'

But four years ago she moved in to Dublin. The papers reported that she was chucked out of Shell Cottage after a rowdy birthday party caused £5,000 worth of damage. She says not so. 'I gave it up because I was lonely. It did have rats. And I'd lived there just long enough. It was self-protection, and there was a moment when it was over. I know the landlord didn't really like me. But you know, a lot of people don't really like me. I'm not everybody's cup of tea!'

I like her for saying that. Unfortunately, liking someone, with me, always provokes a disastrous urge to give good advice, and out it pops. Surely, I tell her, she shouldn't be drinking, surely Hazelden taught her that sobriety was the only salvation? 'I'm not going into all that,' she snaps. And somehow she must have signalled an SOS because suddenly the PR is beside us, telling Marianne, 'I'm really sorry to interrupt, but I do think we need to lead it slightly more to *Intimacy*. I know you've got lots to say about the film.' François simultaneously explodes behind me, 'I knew it! I knew this would happen! It's always the same – this is going to be the last time, Marianne.' 'Why don't you join us, François?' I say, thinking I'd rather have him in sight than shouting over my shoulder, but Marianne says quickly, 'Oh, you don't want that!'

Heroically, like a good Girl Guide, she pulls herself together and starts yacking about *Intimacy* until everyone has calmed down. We both rave about the sex scenes between Kerry Fox and Mark Rylance – she says they remind her of Lucian Freud paintings – she says they're almost like seeing sex for the first time. And, she adds, the orgy scene is brilliant. 'Though of course I've never been to an orgy.' Oh come, Marianne! 'In my mind. I've never actually physically been to an orgy. But it does fascinate me – how do you show decadence onscreen?

And I'm sure that it's not about chandeliers and opulent surroundings, it's exactly like in *Intimacy*. True decadence is an empty room with one bare light bulb.' In the book, she confesses that sex was always her Primal Anxiety. Every 1960s male fantasised about going to bed with the Girl on a Motorcycle – but she suffered terrible stage fright before the act and would do almost anything to put it off. She once spent days hanging around Bob Dylan, seeing off the other groupies, until he finally made his move and then she told him, 'No – I'm pregnant.' Was it performance anxiety? Did she think she was a lousy lay? 'No. I am sexy, we all are – but people saw me as some kind of illusion and I always had a problem with that. But it doesn't really come up any more because, you know, I have a lover and I don't have to worry about it.'

'Who is it?'

'I'm not telling you. I just thought I should explain that when I say I'm not worried about it any more, that doesn't mean I don't have sex any more. It's just not an issue in the sense that one isn't having to take one's clothes off and go to bed with strangers.' Is this a long-term relationship? 'Yes. A deeply committed and serious relationship. But private.' Might they marry? 'I'm not the marrying kind.'

'It is a man, is it?' I blurt, suddenly remembering that her book includes several scenes with women. 'Yes. I'm not gay. I would never rule it out, but it's obviously not my thing – although very nice and perfectly sexy and so on. And anyway I've moved on from that, because I'm in love.'

No amount of questioning from me will yield any more, and she segues smoothly into talking about her life in Dublin.

'I take care of myself. I go swimming. I read a lot. I see my friends. I talk on the phone. I watch telly. I go to bed quite early.' She is scared to live in London because 'it's too on' and she thinks she would be pestered by paparazzi. But she sometimes dreams of having a second home in London so she could see more of her son and grandchildren. She had her only child, Nicholas, when she was just eighteen, and lost custody of him when she became a junkie. But they are on good terms again now. 'I'm really glad I had Nicholas – though I never ever meant to have children. But I had this sort of force that guided me and I knew that if I didn't have Nicholas I'd never have a child – and I never would have, either. But I could see myself going out with my beautiful grown-up son. And I did that last night – we went to see Beck at the Brixton Academy and it was wonderful. I never quite saw the grandchildren!'

Over coffee, I ask her about François. 'Darling François!' she exclaims. 'I'm sorry he's a bit grumpy – he's had so much of it. He's been my manager for seven years.' Just for acting, or for music as well? 'The whole thing. The whole treatment.' She says this almost with a wink and suddenly – how can I have been so slow? – bells ring, scales fall from eyes, and I squeal, aghast, 'Is he The Man?' She says she won't talk about it, but the answer is all too obviously yes. Good God. 'Well, I find him very difficult,' I tell her. 'Yes,' she says, 'but that's partly his job.'

François has obviously been earwigging again, because he suddenly looms over me and shouts, 'Are you talking of me? I hate this fucking tabloid paper. Sex and drugs and all that. I just allowed this interview for Patrice, because

Marianne loves Patrice. If I could put it back, I will.' Marianne hisses at the PR, 'You let him get drunk, you fool.' François, meanwhile, grabs the bill from the waiter and plonks it in front of me. 'Oh,' says Marianne sarcastically, 'is this on the *Observer* – that dreadful tabloid newspaper? Sorry, Lynn.' François shouts at her, 'Don't be sorry, Marianne. Don't apologise. You will see the piece, it will just be sex and drugs, always the same shit. Trust me, for seven years I am telling you the truth.' The PR intervenes brightly, 'I think everything's OK,' only to get a blistering from Marianne: 'Well, no. Everything is not OK. I mean, I'm cool, but François is not pleased. Don't let's go into denial – it's not a river in Egypt.'

So then François snarls some more insults at me and I pay the bill and flounce out. The poor chauffeur is still waiting outside and for a moment I think: Tee hee, I could take the limo home and leave them to grub around for a taxi. But then I think how furious François would be and how he'd take it out on Marianne, and decide I don't really want to punish her quite that much. Though remembering her performance with the waiter I'm fairly torn. I don't for a minute believe in their nice-cop-nasty-cop routine. If François is bad, she's bad too – in fact, maybe worse: she chose him, after all.

Oh, she is exasperating! She is so likeable in some ways but also such a pain. The question that was spinning round my head the whole time was: Who does she think she is? She is a singer with one good album (*Broken English*) to her credit, an actress with one or two good films. Really, her main claim to fame is that she was Mick Jagger's girlfriend in the 1960s, but of course she would never admit that. She thinks she's a great artist who has yet to unleash her full genius on the world. Maybe one day she will, and then I will beg to interview her again on bended knee. Till then, back to the forest, you tiresome old Fabulous Beast.

*

This interview had a strange afterlife in that almost every time Faithfull was interviewed subsequently, the interviewer would mention Lynn Barber and Faithfull would make various disparaging remarks about how aggressive she found me. But *then*, in an Irish interview, she expanded this to claim that I'd asked if she'd ever had sex with a dog. I did *what*? It would never occur to me in a million years to ask if she'd had sex with a dog, because it would never occur to me in a million years that she might have had sex with a dog. Where would I get such an idea? I know I asked about the Mars bar – she said there was no Mars bar and I believed her – but where was this dog supposed to have come from? I was pretty annoyed but I thought: Oh well, she's batty and left it at that. But then she repeated it in another interview and it was in danger of becoming an accepted fact. So I wrote to the editor and said they must print a correction and also warn Faithfull that, if she ever said it again, I would sue her for libel. That might sound a bit heavy, but it could seriously damage my career if it was thought I went around asking people if they had sex with dogs.

Faithfull went silent for a few years – she split from the horrible François, and also suffered breast cancer – but I notice she told the *Irish Times* in February 2011 that she was 'very wild and emotional' when she did that interview and 'I think I might write Lynn a letter to apologise, a letter of amends, for being so rude.' Her letter has yet to turn up, but anyway, no hard feelings, Marianne. The one thing you can say for sure about Marianne Faithfull is that she is not boring.

CHAPTER THREE

On Interviewing

There's a wonderful scene in Jennifer Egan's *A Visit from the Goon Squad* in which an experienced hack called Jules Jones is sent to interview a nineteen-year-old film star called Kitty Jackson over lunch. He has been allotted forty minutes with her of which she spends the first six on her mobile. 'Then she starts to apologise . . . Kitty is sorry for the twelve flaming hoops I've had to jump through and the several miles of piping hot coals I've sprinted across for the privilege of spending forty minutes in her company. She's sorry for having just spent the first six of those minutes talking to somebody else. Her welter of apologies reminds me of why I prefer difficult stars, the ones who barricade themselves inside their stardom and spit through the cracks. There is something out of control about a star who cannot be nice, and the erosion of a subject's self-control is the sine qua non of celebrity reporting.'

That phrase – 'the erosion of a subject's self-control' – pretty much sums up the whole celebrity-interviewing game. But what makes the Jennifer Egan scene so delicious is that it's the reporter who loses his self-control. He gets so irritated by the film star's bland boring niceness that he suggests they go for a walk in Central Park, in the course of which he jumps her, and tries to rape her. He ends up in prison (of course Kitty writes him a sweet letter) charged with attempted rape, kidnapping and aggravated assault. A bit extreme, you might say, but the feelings he goes through while 'trying to wrest readable material from a nineteen-year-old girl who is very, very nice' are ones that I entirely recognise. I have never wanted to rape an interviewee but I have occasionally fantasised that someone else comes in and shoots them. At least then I'd have something to write about.

People often say, 'Oh it must be great for you meeting all these famous people,' and I have to resist the temptation to bang my head on the wall and howl. I dare say it's nice *meeting* famous people but the trouble is I have to interview them which is a completely different kettle of fish. In fact the interview is the part of my job I enjoy least, so fraught is it with anxiety, impatience, frustration, and often disappointment. It's like sitting an exam with not enough time – the clock in my head is ticking so loudly I'm surprised the interviewee can't hear it. I love preparing for an interview, and then writing it up afterwards, but the hour or two I spend with my subject is pretty much pure hell.

The best bit is definitely the research beforehand, especially reading cuttings. It's the perfect combination of limitless displacement activity with what one can tell oneself is work – 'I'm sorry I have to lie on the sofa all day but I have to read all these cuttings.' Nowadays I have to read them on my laptop which is not nearly so much fun, but I used to love getting real yellowing cuttings in real dusty brown files from the Tasiemka Archive in Golders Green. Edda Tasiemka, a German émigré, used to help her journalist husband by cutting out articles she thought might be useful for him.

When he died she went on cutting out articles till her entire house was crammed floor to ceiling – not just the sitting room and bedrooms but hall, bathroom, kitchen, landing, garage – with bulging brown files. She's still doing it, aged ninety, but alas now editors balk at paying her fees and say you can find it all on the internet. You can't, actually. You can't hold in your hands the actual *Sun* front page that screamed 'Freddie Starr ate my hamster' whereas you can at Mrs Tasiemka's. I still sometimes go round to her house just for the joy of riffling through old cuttings.

The point of background research is that you don't waste precious interview minutes asking for information you could have found out beforehand, such as where they grew up or went to school. But it's also useful to read previous interviews because they give you a clue as to what you're in for – if your subject has *never* produced a good quote, you know you'll be ploughing stony ground. And if you find the same anecdotes recurring in interview after interview you know these are the ones to avoid.

But the most valuable part of reading the cuttings is looking for the lacunae – the things that *haven't* been talked about. Researching the actor Dan Stevens, I was struck by how little he'd said about being adopted. He had a short standard answer to the effect that he didn't want to know about his 'real' parents, he was not interested, because his adoptive parents had been so wonderful. In fact he resented the suggestion that they were less 'real' than his genetic parents. But, now that he is a father himself, I felt he *must* want to know about his genetic parents, and asked if he'd found out anything more. He said no – he'd been too busy to do any research – but then admitted that he knew more than he was ever willing to divulge. Fair enough. To say yes, I know the facts but I'm not telling is an honest answer whereas I'm not interested is not.

Again, doing background research for an interview with Piers Morgan, I wondered why he'd never talked about his real father. He was a dentist, name of O'Meara (Piers switched to his stepfather's name), who died when Piers was a baby. But why did he die so young? Piers said it was 'nothing sinister' but flatly refused to tell me the cause of death. I suppose you could say that this was an interviewing failure – I drew a blank – but I certainly felt it was worth including in the article. On occasions like this, I often feel that I'm marking the spot for future interviewers to dig.

Reading cuttings is such a pleasure I can easily do it for days. There might also be a biography or autobiography I have to read, or films I have to watch, or records I have to listen to, not to mention YouTube and Twitter and a million other distractions that I can tell myself are necessary for my research. I like to feel I am thoroughly prepared – it gives me confidence on the day. But, come the day, I wake with a racing heart and a feeling of doom. I always try to arrange interviews for the morning so I have less time to worry. I do all the routine stuff – checking my tape recorder, checking the batteries, rereading my notes, rereading my questions, checking the address, but then there is nothing to do except panic and wonder whether I will screw up.

There are a million ways of screwing up and I must have done them all at one time or another. Arriving late is the most obvious one though I'm such a punctuality freak it has very rarely happened. Having a tape recorder break down is another horror but nowadays I always take two recorders just in case. The worst breakdown ever was with Sir David Attenborough – I saw the light flickering and realised my batteries were fading, but he was NOT sympathetic. Consequently while everyone else reveres him as a national treasure, I can only remember the cold glint in his eye, the drumming fingers, while I fiddled cack-handedly with my batteries.

Of course, I always fear a physical crisis and it's happened a couple of times – once with Oliver Stone, when my front tooth (crown) fell out, but actually he was very kind and sympathetic, and another time with Robert Redford when I had a coughing fit so bad it sounded like retching. He sat there with a bottle of water beside him, failing to offer me any – his stony face indicated that he was furious I might be giving him germs. I remember sweating hideously in a conservatory with the actor William Hurt and him passing me ice cubes to cool my bright red face. He meant it kindly, I'm sure, but I wouldn't have known my face was bright red unless he'd drawn my attention to it.

But even without any physical crisis, or tape-recorder crisis, there are still a million things that can go wrong – often just pacing things badly, or failing to follow up an interesting lead, or forgetting to ask a crucial question. My problem always is impatience. I'm prone to rush the early stages, desperate to get on to the meat of the interview. But it is vital to let the interviewee settle down and relax before asking anything that might alarm them. Which means that you must let them do the plug – and nowadays there always IS a plug – for their film or book or record, before you get on to the interesting stuff about why they've just split from their fifth wife. I tell myself I mustn't push for *anything* in the first fifteen minutes; I must let them fulfil their agenda and say the things they have probably been reciting in the bathroom mirror before I make any attempt to steer the interview.

I used to devote a lot of thought to what to wear to the interview because I wanted to 'blend in'. If I was interviewing an Establishment figure, I wore a Sloaney suit; if I was interviewing an actor, I aimed for something more bohemian; if I was interviewing a footballer – ah, there was the rub, because how do you dress to fit in with a footballer? I think it was probably wasted effort anyway, and nowadays my clothes are so much of a muchness I don't have the wardrobe to dress like a Sloane. Anyway, how on earth would I dress to 'blend in' with, say, Shane MacGowan or Lady Gaga? Shane MacGowan had vomit encrusted all down his trousers, Lady Gaga was wearing a black silk wrap that kept falling open to show her bare boobs.

My only rule is not to wear anything that looks too expensive because I don't want to seem to be showing off. I remember the first time I interviewed Sir Alan Sugar (at his hideous house in Boca Raton) he pointed to my emerald ring and asked, 'How much did that cost?' I said rather snottily that it was my engagement ring so I had no idea, but he said, 'Go on – guess.' 'Five grand?' I ventured. 'They wouldn't give you five hundred for it down Hatton Garden,' he told me in my first full blast of the famous Sugar charm. *He* obviously thought I wore it to show off.

Actually my engagement ring had drawn attention once before, when I interviewed Ronnie Biggs the Great Train

Robber in Rio de Janeiro in 1984. I was waiting for him at his flat and talking to his girlfriend Ulla when she suddenly seized my hand and said, 'My dear, I must tell you: you must never ever wear a ring like that in Rio. The thieves here are terrible. They would cut off your finger to get it. And there are thieves everywhere here in Rio.' Just as she said it, Ronnie Biggs, the most famous thief in Rio, walked through the door!

Ideally, you should always interview people at home because you can learn so much about them. Are they super-neat or chaotic? Do they have more photographs of their family or of themselves? A trip to the loo is often instructive – it's where people put their awards and cartoons – things they're proud of and want visitors to see but without too obviously showing off. Of course if you can go to their own bathroom, rather than the guest cloakroom, better still – look for the pills! Liz Jones, the *Mail* columnist, told me that she always headed for the bathroom – she also went through David Cassidy's wheelie bin when she interviewed him in Los Angeles but then she is a far more committed journalist than me.

Nowadays, of course, the question of smoking looms large. Even before the smoking ban, I made it a rule not to smoke in people's houses unless they were smokers themselves, but at least in those days you could smoke in restaurants. But now my preparation for any interview includes donning the hated nicotine patch – and then great whoops of delight if the person turns out to be a fellow smoker. I remember interviewing Simon Cowell at his headquarters and thinking even *he* won't be allowed to smoke in this immaculate building, but he immediately produced cigs, lighter, ashtray from his desk drawer and we both merrily puffed away. Some of my friendliest interviews have been done on the smoking pavement outside restaurants – I did one with Rhys Ifans supposedly over lunch where we spent maybe twenty minutes in the restaurant and two hours outside.

An interview is an odd transaction – just two people alone in a room, with a tape recorder. It looks like an intimate tête-à-tête but you both know that it's 'on the record', intended for publication. On the other hand, you don't *speak* as if to an audience. It feels – or should do – as if you are having a rather intense private conversation. That's one reason why I think it's so important to maintain eye contact at all times. I'm baffled by interviewers (invariably men) who ask questions while flicking through their notebook, or glancing round the room.

Outsiders inevitably derive their idea of what interviews are like from watching them on television without realising that press interviews are completely different. Broadcast interviews have to include lots of information in the questions, because there is no other place to put it, therefore the questions have to be to some extent pre-planned. But press interviews aren't like that because the questions don't need to carry any information. They just have to be as effective as possible at getting the subject to talk. Hopefully, the questions will always be much shorter than the answer – my absolute favourite question is always: Why? If an interviewee says that he decided to move away from London a couple of years ago, this is not of any great interest until you interject 'Why?' and it all comes tumbling out – 'Oh you know, because I was spending too much time getting pissed in the Groucho and ending up in bed with people whose names I couldn't remember in the morning.' So that's a cue to ask: What was the worst occasion?

And then, with any luck, the interview has moved from mildly interesting into riveting.

People sometimes claim that doing an interview is almost like psychotherapy. That's obvious nonsense because there is no therapeutic intent. But I have sometimes been accused of coming on 'like a therapist' – most memorably by Anne Robinson who was very contemptuous of the vagueness of my questions. She would have rattled them out rat-a-tat-tat, each one spikier than the last. But then would she have got such a good interview? By slowing things down, refusing to engage in the sort of verbal sparring Robinson wanted, I think I got more out of her than she meant to give. She was more rattled by soft questions than by tough ones.

I want my questions to be as open-ended as possible. The aim is not to produce tick-box answers – Happy childhood? Yes. Good relations with mother? Yes. Father? Yes. Siblings? Yes. The open-ended version would be: Who were you closest to during your childhood? The answer is usually mother or father, but if it's not – if it's sister or granny or auntie, it is worth probing a bit more. And of course I *am* like a therapist in that I always ask about childhood. I feel if I can picture what my interviewee was like at seven, at fourteen, I am much closer to understanding who they are today.

It goes without saying that I am entirely reliant on tape recorders – having no memory and having long forgotten my shorthand, I couldn't have been an interviewer if they hadn't been invented. Some people argue that recorders make interviewees nervous, but I think that only lasts for the first five minutes provided you maintain eye contact. And I like the formality of producing my recorder at the beginning of an interview, choosing the right place to put it, testing it, all as a way of demonstrating, 'Right. This is an interview. We are now on the record.' And then, at the end, a sign-off whereby, hand hovering above the recorder, I say, 'Well thank you for that. But is there anything you would like to raise that I haven't given you a chance to talk about?' Usually the answer is no and then I ostentatiously click the recorder off and put it in my bag. If it's yes, then obviously I carry on recording till they've said whatever they wanted to say. But the whole business of displaying the tape recorder is for me an important way of reminding the subject that we are not having a chat, we are doing an interview, for publication.

Even so, people sometimes want to say something off the record and this is a dilemma. I really hate being told things off the record – it makes life difficult when it comes to writing the piece. Jeffrey Archer, who I interviewed back in the 1980s when he was Conservative Party chairman, kept issuing instructions – 'This is off the record'; 'You can say this in your own words but not in mine'; 'You can say "friends of Jeffrey Archer told me" '. All these supposedly off-the-record revelations were entirely self-serving, designed to convey what a wonderful chap he was without too obviously boasting – though I must say boasting was not normally a problem for him. Journalists who feel flattered by being told things off the record are wet behind the ears. Nobody ever tells you anything that would harm them. They never say, 'By the way, I *did* murder my wife'; they say, 'Off the record, my wife was mad as a snake and a complete lush. I nursed her devotedly for many years until she had that unfortunate fall down the stairs.' I often say at the beginning of an interview that *everything* is on the record – by which I mean including anything they try to tell me off the record. I would simply rather not know – or find it out myself by other means.

The great disadvantage of recording interviews is that you then have to listen to your own voice when you play them back, and oh, how agonising that is! You come to recognise, all too well, your own verbal tics and mannerisms and of course this is the moment when you think of all the questions you forgot to ask, or the points where you should have butted in and asked for more explication. Younger, cleverer journalists tend to save themselves this agony by using a transcription service or one of the wizard computer programmes that can convert speech into writing, but my attempts at both have been useless, and anyway I quite value the time spent transcribing the tape. It's when I really think about the subject and what I want to say about them. It's also when I identify the quotes I will definitely use in the piece, and others that are good but not essential.

Given my devotion to recorders, I am amazed when I encounter journalists who don't use them. However brilliant their shorthand, there must be one or two points where the shorthand is ambiguous, when it would be helpful to have a recording to check. Also I think editors should insist on recording – it's good insurance, if anyone ever claims they've been misquoted. Actually, I think *interviewees* should use recorders as well – why not? Michael Winner and Tony Benn always did, but I wish it were general practice. I get fed up with interviewees telling me they were misquoted, when I read them something from the cuttings. If they were really misquoted, then why didn't they complain at the time? And if not, then why are they slandering a journalist by saying that they were?

The other great virtue of recorders is that they allow you to quote someone's words *exactly* and not just the gist. In fact this seems to me the whole joy of interviews – to capture people's way of speaking. Do they speak disjointedly, or do they form complete sentences? Do they repeat themselves? Do they have favourite words they use far too much? ('Basically' is a big offender here.) Do they use those giveaway phrases 'to be perfectly frank' or 'I must be honest with you' which always suggest they've been lying the rest of the time? Or, worst of all, do they say 'know what I mean' because if they say it at all, they will tend to say it in every sentence. The boxer Frank Bruno was a nightmare in that respect; ditto the musician Goldie. I usually cut most of the 'know what I mean's because they are too boring to read, but it's important to include a couple to convey their ubiquity.

'Fucking' is another problem. Actually it's a really acute problem for me now I work for the *Sunday Times* because they insist on following the antique practice of filling the word with asterisks. It didn't happen before, when I worked for the *Independent on Sunday* and the *Observer*, but the *Sunday Times* considers itself a 'family newspaper'. This is of course insane because if children ever scan the paper, it's the word with asterisks that will first catch their eye. When I interviewed Lady Gaga, she discussed, among other things, the size of her clitoris, but nevertheless it was her one use of the word 'fucking' that had to be bowdlerised.

How can you accurately quote people who use 'fucking' every other word? With Liam Gallagher I was able to make it 'fooking' because that was the way he pronounced it, but with David Bailey I had to cut nearly all his 'fucking's out, which I thought was a loss. I did an interview with Norman Mailer in 1998 (luckily, for the *Observer*, which had no silly rules about asterisks) which almost hinged on his use – no, *my* use – of the word 'fuck'. He'd been a bit torpid before, very deaf, very old, very arthritic, but he was *thrilled* when I asked him if he thought women should have babies as a souvenir of a great fuck. Obviously he got a kick out of hearing that word on the lips of (he thought) a genteel Englishwoman and from then on he kept using the word 'fuck' in almost every sentence – 'Great fucks are very rare! Great fucks are rare enough that they have to be respected!' And, yes, he did think that women should have babies as souvenirs of great fucks.

I go into interviews armed first and foremost with a recorder but also with a long list of prepared questions. I don't often refer to them but they are vital to cover those moments, which happen in every interview, when my mind goes blank. And I put an asterisk by the questions I absolutely *must* ask, because I will be a wimp if I don't. An interviewer can't afford to be shy about asking questions – it's what you're there for. I always tell my interviewees beforehand that they mustn't mind if I ask an intrusive question – they can always shake their head and say 'No comment'. I won't press it – I won't do a Paxman and repeat the question twelve times. But it's daft not to ask.

A question I am fond of is: What do you think is your worst fault? Nobody ever, of course, really admits what their worst fault is (nor would I) but there is a difference between people who say, for instance, unpunctuality or forgetting names, i.e. they admit to *some* fault although not by any means a serious one, and people who turn it into a self-compliment by saying, 'Oh my worst fault is that I'm too giving!' Yeah? At this point I always want to ask: How much do you pay your cleaner (I always want to ask *everyone* how much they pay their cleaner) but I have to fight back the urge, and ask something more anodyne like: Could you give me an example?

Asking for examples is always fruitful. It's no good talking in generalisations when what you desperately need is detail. I do believe that detail is everything. Detail is evidence. When I interviewed the novelist Lionel Shriver, she obviously thought I was mad to keep asking about her central heating. But I was trying to nail my hunch that she was frugal and ascetic to the point of masochism, and I needed the evidence – which indeed she delivered. She told me that she prefers to wear a coat and gloves indoors rather than have the heating on, even though she suffers from Raynaud's disease which means her hands and feet are always cold, and she will only let her husband switch the heating on if it is actually freezing outside, but then not until 7 p.m. That surely should be enough to convince the reader. Shriver told me off afterwards for being so obsessed with her heating and emailed, 'The frequency with which I turn on the central heating may not loom large in the world of letters years hence!' True – but as an insight into her character, I think her central-heating habits are quite significant.

Some beginner journalists, especially men, I think, have difficulty with the 'stance' of interviews – they find it obscurely humiliating to be taking all this interest in someone else without getting any reciprocal interest back. They hope that an interview will be a meeting of minds, or, alternatively, a debate. It should not be. An interview is not the time to show off, or to express your own opinions. You are there to draw someone out, to get *their* views, *their* memories, hopefully *their* confessions, and the less you talk yourself, the better. Outsiders often don't realise how constrained by time most interviews are. Nowadays you're lucky to get any more than an hour with your subject. So any minute spent talking about yourself is a minute wasted. I remember years ago Julie Andrews, being friendly, asked if I had children and I said no. I knew that if I said I had two daughters she'd start asking their names and ages and five minutes would have gone. But also I think you are more effective as an interviewer if you divulge as little of yourself as possible.

To be a good interviewer you have to know yourself pretty well, and obviously age is an advantage here. To some extent I use myself as a sounding-board. I know how I normally feel, so if I come out of an interview feeling atypically depressed, or humiliated, or elated, I know it must be something my interviewee has said or done to make me feel that way. So when I transcribe the tape, I try to identify the moment when my mood changed, and what triggered it. I believe that emotions are to some extent catching, so I know that a depressed person will make me feel depressed, and an angry person will make me angry. The reason my interview with Martin Clunes (see next chapter) ended so badly was, I think, because he was seething with repressed anger from the beginning, and increasingly his anger transferred itself to me.

You can never hope to do a 'definitive' interview because interviews, by their very nature, are of the moment, and at the mercy of happenstance. You can convey what someone was like on the day you met them, but they can be very different on different days. When I interviewed the actor Rhys Ifans in 2011 I found him amusing, pleasant, sharply intelligent, and willing to talk candidly about his love life and his hopes of fatherhood. But Janice Turner interviewed him for *The Times* two years later and found him boorish, foul-mouthed and unwilling to answer any questions at all. Her Rhys Ifans was the exact opposite of mine. So was I wrong and she right? Was he putting on an act for me? Or was he, as his publicist said, suffering from 'a bad reaction to antibiotics' on the day Janice Turner met him? I don't think there's any clear-cut explanation. Rhys Ifans no doubt has different moods on different days – as we all do, but perhaps actors more than most – and I caught one mood and Janice Turner another. But that's the joy of interviews – their infinite variety.

CHAPTER FOUR

Actors

Oh God, actors are difficult to interview. The trouble is they're so fluent. They babble away unstoppably and you think you've got some quite interesting stuff, but when you transcribe the tape, and strip out all the funny accents, and the expressive gestures and the whole actory *business*, you realise you're left with some very stale old anecdotes, which might work fine on a television chat show, but not on the page.

I should also confess that I have some psychological 'issues' with actors, stemming from my childhood. My mother had dreamed of being an actress but trained as an elocution teacher instead, so all her hopes of a thespian career were loaded on to me. She dragged me round poetry reading competitions from a very early age – I always hated them because I never won. But whereas she kept hoping I'd win next time, I recognised quite early on that I didn't deserve to win, that there were people who were better than me and far more committed. But still my mother wouldn't give up.

She was a big cheese in Richmond amateur dramatics and often found small parts for me in her productions so I spent a lot of time as a young teenager sitting quietly in the dressing room while actors carried on – and they did carry on – around me. It was almost like bird-watching – I could see these dramas unfold without ever being expected to participate. I observed then, and believe still, that actors almost by definition have to be self-deluding. They live in this strange optimistic bubble where they are still hoping to play Juliet in their fifties (of course in Richmond amateur dramatics circles they sometimes did) or believe they will be discovered by a great Hollywood producer while they are playing fourth spear-carrier from the left. They keep the whole bubble afloat by telling each other they are wonderful, darling, when quite patently they are not. I hated the whole falseness of it and it upset me that my mother fell for these delusions. I wanted to say, 'Look, why can't you be realistic like me and Dad, why do you fill your head with this mush?' Theatre was like a lover who lured her away from us and I resented it. So that is why I have a problem with actors.

And having a problem with actors is quite a big problem in my job because there are so *many* of them – hardly a week passes in which I am not offered an interview with the latest hot new thing, and when all other efforts fail, it is very easy to fall back on them. And then they tell you that really they're very shy, and playing this role is like climbing Everest, and you want to bang your head on the wall and scream, 'Shut UP!'

I also find it difficult to tell which actors are any good – I have to take other people's word for it. I never go to the theatre. (Was it Martin Amis who said why go to the theatre when you can stand on a street corner in the rain and watch the cars go by? My feelings precisely.) Consequently I never know their 'work' or, basically, what they are talking about. Obviously if they've made films, I can watch them on DVD, but I still don't really know why some actors are considered good and others rubbish – it all seems much of a muchness to me, unless they're so bad they're funny.

All journalists dread the hotel circus, when a film company puts a herd of actors in a hotel for a day to plug their new film and expects them to give interviews from dawn to dusk. The journalists are corralled in one suite, a sort of holding pen, with pots of cooling coffee and stale buns, and then led out one by one for their allotted ten or fifteen minutes with the star, with the proviso that they also have to interview the lesser fry along the corridor later. There's a fairly accurate scene of a hotel circus in the film *Notting Hill*, where Hugh Grant is given ten minutes to interview Julia Roberts with a PR breathing down his neck – except the big inaccuracy is that he is given ten minutes when he is only meant to be from *Horse & Hound*.

The other problem with actors on these publicity treadmills is that they're often talking about a film they made two or more years ago, which they've almost forgotten. Sometimes they've made three or four more films since then, and often they've made a better film which is the one they want to talk about – which is precisely why there is a PR sitting in the room to prevent them doing that.

They are so zonked by doing non-stop interviews that often they will repeat an anecdote they've already told you word for word, or else start an anecdote and then forget the ending. Often they have no idea what country they are in. At least twice (once with Audrey Hepburn, once with Lynn Redgrave)

I've felt that my interviewee was so exhausted and emotionally fragile I really should be calling an ambulance rather than asking questions. But still the PR sits there stony-faced, forcing these poor knackered ponies to jump through their publicity hoops.

The only question I've found that occasionally works in these hotel circuses is to ask the actor what they would be doing if they were at home this minute. Of course they are so disoriented you often have to tell them what time of day it is, but you are sometimes rewarded with a rush of homesickness, and they will talk nostalgically about collecting the kids or going to their yoga class or taking flying lessons, which at least gives you a glimpse into their real lives. But then the PR cracks the whip and they are back to talking about their wretched film.

And of course it's an article of faith that they never slag off the director, or other actors – everyone they work with is always 'wonderful', at least while they are plugging the film. I've found a fairly fruitful question is: Which other actor on the film did you most admire, or most enjoy working with? Invariably they nominate someone who had such a tiny part you never even noticed them. (Though when I interviewed Robert Redford about *The Horse Whisperer* he couldn't bring himself to praise *any* of his fellow actors, not even the horse.) So then you ask: What about your co-star? And they go into a predictable rap about what a joy it was to work with Meryl/Judi/Jessica, whoever. At this point, it's time to get down to the nitty-gritty: Which of you knew your lines best? And you can see doubt and confusion spread across their perfect features, as they struggle between the Scylla of saying that *of course* they knew their lines best, and the Charybdis of dissing a fellow actor. Eventually they arrive at the formula 'we all knew our lines perfectly' but it can take a long time.

Another good question is: Who did you have dinner with most nights on location? They daren't say their co-star because it would sound as if they were having an affair; on the other hand, they don't like to say their stunt double because it sounds as if they're gay. Safest answer is the director – though actually the last thing most directors want is to spend evenings with their actors. The truthful answer is probably with room service but again, they don't like to say that because it sounds pathetic.

Basically, there is almost no way into the inner life of actors and God knows I've tried. But it's maddening because I think that, even if their personalities are dull, their lifestyles are hugely interesting. I like the fact that they're essentially nomads, prepared to go almost anywhere for a part, who will spend weeks or even months in some backwoods town in Romania or Newfoundland where I will never go. But when you ask them what Newfoundland was like, they start talking about the bloody role, and it's obvious they've never noticed Newfoundland. I suppose it's inevitable: they get collected from their hotel before dawn, and driven to the location, back after sunset, they probably only have the vaguest idea what country they are in.

But because actors are so international they're often in the vanguard of all the latest trends. I remember Oliver Stone telling me about sweat lodges and Ayurvedic medicine long before these were common currency, and Ruby Wax showing me her Notting Hill house done up in 'Sante Fe style' before I'd even heard of such a thing. I saw my first-ever glass wash-basin in Elaine Paige's penthouse. There is often a time lag of two or three years before such innovations begin appearing in the style magazines. And of course actors are always up to speed with the latest forms of psychobabble and rehab-speak which I always enjoy hearing.

I can't now remember who was the first actor I ever inter-viewed, but I do vividly remember my first trip to Hollywood in 1983. It was to interview the actor James Stewart, who was seventy-five and long retired, but Universal Studios was reis-suing four of his major Hitchcock films – *Rope*, *Vertigo*, *Rear Window* and *The Man Who Knew Too Much* – which had been suppressed at Alfred Hitchcock's request for twenty years. (One theory about why Hitchcock withdrew them was to keep them off television.) The studio paid for my trip which was fabulous – first-class flight to Los Angeles, limo to meet me, suite at the Bel-Air Hotel – but when I arrived there was a note from the studio to say that unfortunately Mr Stewart had a slight cold and would like to postpone the interview till the day after tomorrow. Fine by me.

The PR rang and asked how I would like to spend my free time, and I said I'd like to see Los Angeles, and he said of course the limo was at my disposal, so I spent an idyllic day being driven round Los Angeles. I asked to go to Venice Beach and the chauffeur seemed a bit reluctant – he said that last time he'd been there he was driving a famous director's chil-dren, and they'd seen a man shot dead as soon as they arrived. The children loved it apparently, but the driver was pretty shaken. The next day the interview was postponed again – Mr

Stewart was still ill – so the PR suggested I go on the Universal Studios tour which was good fun, seeing the *Psycho* house and all the rest of it.

Eventually Mr Stewart was fit for interview and I went to his house in Beverly Hills. I must say the house was disappointing – a sort of Tudorbethan Agatha Christie job that could just as well have been in Esher. But he was as lovely as everyone said he would be. He was rather deaf and of course famously slow-talking, so he didn't exactly gush away but he talked fondly about his father, who kept a hardware store. His father came to stay with him in Hollywood after the war and asked, 'Where do you go to church around here?' James Stewart confessed he didn't think there was a Presbyterian church around there so his father went for a walk and came back forty-five minutes later with four men who were elders of the Presbyterian church. They explained that they didn't have a church building, but they had a minister and a congregation and they held services in private homes. 'Wa . . . all,' said Mr Stewart, 'to make a long story short, I ended up helping to build that church, and Gloria and I were married in that church.'

Towards the end, I raised the question of when he would do photographs. The studio had been pussy-footing on this, never giving a straight answer. Mr Stewart explained that he was awaiting a new hairpiece, and he couldn't be photographed till it was fitted. (This might have been the reason he postponed the interview.) But, I told him, he looked fine without it. Yes, he said, but he looked *old*. But, but – how could I frame this tactfully? – given that he was seventy-five, who could really expect him to look young? 'Fans,' he said soberly. 'It upsets the fans. They want you to look exactly as they remember you. If you look old, it makes *them* feel old. It is unkind, it is *selfish*, to let oneself go.'

It turned out that he wasn't willing to do photographs at all, and when I persisted, he turned suddenly grouchy and said, 'The studio must have photographs, what *happened* to all those photographs? I can't be expected to sit around all the time doing head shots, I just won't do it.' So afterwards I asked the studio if they had any recent photographs of Jimmy Stewart, preferably without his toupee. I might have said without his clothes on, they were so shocked. 'Without his lid on? Oh no. He IS a star, you know.' James Stewart himself once said of being a star, 'I take it as a sort of responsibility,' and for him it seems that responsibility included not only keeping his private life immaculate, but also never allowing himself to be photographed without a toupee. We used an old studio portrait in the end.

Dirk Bogarde gave me a similar lecture about the need to maintain film-star standards. When I interviewed him in 1987 he had stopped being a film star and had forged an excellent new career as a writer. Consequently I expected him to behave like a writer – but he didn't, he was still a film star. He insisted on having a chauffeur-driven limo deliver him to Claridge's for tea, where the Penguin publicist would be on hand to greet him and his personal publicist would sit in on the interview.

He told me that when he did his first book publicity tour for Chatto, they were gob-smacked at the expense. 'But I was a film star and I wanted what I'd always had – the black limo, the best hotels, everything on the dot, and every door opened for me so that I would never, ever be late. The publishers couldn't twig it *at all*. I warned them. When Lauren Bacall came over to publicise her book, I said, "Look, she's not *used* to sitting in the back of the rep's car with a lot of dirty nappies. She wants the full treatment." Of course, they didn't believe me – until they sent the Datsun and she simply refused to get in.'

But why do you have to be like that, I wailed – is it just vanity? 'No, because it's more efficient that way. And image *counts* – of course it does. It doesn't matter to *me* if I travel in the rep's car, but it does matter to the public who expect you to arrive like Cinderella in a coach. They're disappointed if you don't.'

Ah, the public, the public. Who *are* these mysterious people? They never seem to include me, or anyone I know. And yet actors are forever talking about the public, or even *their* public, these anonymous cohorts of little people whose very happiness depends on seeing their stars in toupees and limousines. I notice that pop stars, artists, writers don't do it – they might talk about their fans, but they never claim ownership of this mysterious entity 'the public'. I asked Dirk Bogarde: What is the role of the journalist in all this? To puncture the image or to sustain it?

'I never know *what* the role of the journalist is,' he sighed.

I don't either, but one thing I've long suspected is that all actors secretly hate journalists. This was confirmed to me when I interviewed Martin Clunes.

This is the story of a love affair and its ending. My love affair was with *Doc Martin*, the ITV series about a brilliant surgeon who has to resign his hospital job when he develops a phobia about blood, and moves to a Cornish village (Portwenn in the script; Port Isaac in reality) to become a GP. The first series went out in 2004, and there have been four more since, but I only discovered it about a year ago, and caught up on DVDs. At first it was my guilty secret but then I asked a few friends if they'd ever seen it. No, was the sniffy answer, often accompanied by some hurtful remark on the lines of, 'But I do sometimes watch *Poirot*.' *Poirot* indeed!

So then I casually asked on Twitter whether anyone apart from me loved *Doc Martin* and was bombarded with tweets for days. It turns out there are millions of *Doc Martin* fans, not just the nine million who watch it here, but millions more in the US, Canada, Australia and New Zealand. They make little YouTube compilations of their favourite *Doc Martin* clips and discuss whether the doctor and Louisa can find lasting happiness. There is even a docmartinstore website offering *Doc Martin* toffee and blood-effect mouse mats and mugs saying 'Stop talking' and 'Make an appointment'.

I must confess I found my sudden entry into the huggy bosom of the *Doc Martin* 'community' a tad bewildering, but even more so was the fact that my old friends, who had been so snooty before, simultaneously started saying they were now converts to *Doc Martin*. Why? 'Because Eileen Atkins is so wonderful in it.' Oh tsk, of all the reasons for watching *Doc Martin*, this is the most egregious! Atkins arrived at the start of the fifth series, when the scriptwriters killed off the doctor's aunt Joan (Stephanie Cole) who I must say was a dreadful bore, and brought in a different, more spiky and intelligent, aunt to inherit her house. The arrival of a posh thespian like Eileen Atkins apparently means it's now acceptable to talk about *Doc Martin* at dinner parties.

But of course what makes *Doc Martin* wonderful (apart from the brilliant script, the gorgeous Cornish setting, and all the exciting diseases we'll get on to later) is Martin Clunes as the doctor. I always assumed when he was Gary in *Men Behaving Badly* that he was just playing himself, but I realise from *Doc Martin* that he's one of the finest, subtlest television actors around. *Doc Martin* is the complete opposite of Gary – uptight, unsmiling, abrasive, brutally rude to his patients and unfailingly rough with children.

So anyway, this was a happy prospect, going to interview an actor I genuinely admire, and to talk about my favourite television show. And it all started so well. His house, surrounded by horses and lambs, is on a beautiful Dorset hillside with views right down to the Jurassic Coast. While Clunes poses for photographs, his wife Philippa Braithwaite, who produces *Doc Martin*, makes me coffee in the Smeg-filled kitchen and lets me admire all the family photographs – Martin, Philippa and daughter Emily, twelve – and portraits of their many dogs and horses.

So far, so good, and even better when Martin Clunes appears, in a great whoosh of dogs, and ushers me through to the sitting room to talk. He is smiling, laughing, jovial, friendly. Everyone – even my colleague Camilla Long – has told me I will love him. He raves on about a visit he and

Philippa have just made to the Army Saddle Club in Cyprus, in his capacity as President of the British Horse Society, and what fun it was meeting Army families and talking horse. He points proudly through the window to his enormous steed Chester, and says they have another fourteen horses and some miniature Shetland ponies in the paddocks. He gets up at 6.30 to feed them all, and has spent the morning moving lambs up the hill. He calls himself 'a luvvie farmer' but he obviously takes his farming seriously.

This bucolic chat is all very well, but I am dying to talk about *Doc Martin*. Unfortunately, Martin Clunes doesn't seem to be. He says he wants more roles, different roles, he wants to do more acting. 'Of course *Doc Martin* is acting, but it's a particular kind of job because it's our own company [Buffalo Pictures] that makes it, so it's just very different from a normal actor's life.' He found a few years ago that he was no longer being offered parts, which is why he made TV documentaries (produced by Philippa) about dogs and horses and islands. But his first love is still acting. 'I really want to get back to acting. I went up for a job last week – I didn't get it. But I thought: Great! This is what I signed up for, you know. To actually go up for a part and they say choose some scenes to read, I really found it refreshing. I'm kind of sad that I don't do it any more.'

But this is so disloyal to *Doc Martin*! Could he seriously contemplate doing a different television series? 'Why not? I'm self-employed. Yes. I just want to do something else as well, that's why I'm going to all these auditions. I want to go back to supporting and not having the whole thing on my shoulders, playing the title role. Because I'm basically a character actor who got lucky, you know. And I'm sort of preparing for the twilight of my career. I'm fifty and there's no guarantee, no pension. And if you're self-employed, you always worry about that.' But he can't seriously worry about money – his farm must be worth a fortune. 'Yes indeed – that's where all the money went! But I just need to do what I do. I only realised this year that I really miss acting.'

Dearohdearohdearohdear. Luckily he has signed up for one more series of *Doc Martin*, the sixth, but he insists that will be the last. Sob. 'It would just be such a contortion to carry on. It would get repetitive, it would become a soap. And we can't keep the will-they-won't-they thing going with Louisa now they're together. They have to co-exist – though at what level of functionality, I don't know.'

Another problem is that they must sooner or later run out of diseases. The inhabitants of Portwenn have suffered from every obscure ailment known to medicine. They develop arsenic poisoning from their wallpaper; they grow breasts from ingesting their wife's HRT cream, or break their legs from taking too many calcium supplements. And they frequently 'go Bodmin' from, say, cleaning their floors with weedkiller the way they do. (The Mayor of Bodmin objected to the use of 'gone Bodmin' in the script but actually it's widespread in Cornwall because Bodmin used to have the county's biggest mental hospital.) The very first time Doc Martin saw Louisa he looked deep into her eyes – and told her she had glaucoma. But glaucoma is a very minor ailment by Portwenn standards.

The diseases are supplied by Dr Martin Scurr who acts as

medical adviser. He was enlisted right at the beginning by scriptwriter Dominic Minghella (brother of the late Anthony) who asked him to suggest some rare diseases to show off Doc Martin's skill as a diagnostician, and he came up with the man who grew breasts in the very first episode. Scurr takes his job very seriously and rides down to Port Isaac on his motorbike any time Doc Martin has to undertake a new procedure. 'First time I defribbed,' Clunes recalls, 'first time I delivered a baby, he was there.' Scurr gets furious when screen medics do things wrong – examining a patient from the left-hand side of the bed instead of the right, or 'that terrible ear examination in *We Need to Talk about Kevin*'. *Doc Martin* generally gets high marks from the medical profession (unlike *House*) and some of the episodes have been used as teaching aids, but there was a bit of flak in the last series when Eileen Atkins told Doc Martin that she was dying of lupus. Doc Martin examined her and said no she didn't have lupus, she had Sjogren's syndrome – but he failed to correct the idea that lupus was necessarily fatal.

Martin Clunes has often said that the reason he likes playing Doc Martin is because he finds it exhilarating to be so rude – 'It's my liberation from having to be nice to people.' He claims he is by nature emollient and eager to please. Nevertheless I sense an underlying irritability and he admits that he can have a temper if annoyed. But rather than shout at people, he withdraws. 'Nowadays I think: Oh I don't have to put up with that, and I'll just extricate myself from the situation. Whereas I used to put up with it silently.'

His father, the actor Alec Clunes, always seemed a rather tortured soul and had a reputation for not suffering fools gladly. Martin says he didn't really know his father because he died when he was eight but, 'I keep finding things out about him as I get older. Yes, I think he probably was quite tortured. I think he gave a lot of people quite a hard time. He was a bit of a prick actually. I don't think he was very nice to my mum.' Martin only found out years later that his father had actually abandoned the family and gone to live in Majorca, but returned a few months later when he was diagnosed with lung cancer.

Nevertheless his mother always claimed that he was a wonderful husband and father. 'Because SHE worshipped him. She was very stage-struck, till her dying day [she died four years ago], and she used to work for him at the Arts Theatre and he was a very serious classical actor. And she would talk about actors and say oh so and so was wonderful in such and such. And I'd say but he was a complete bastard who hit his wife and she would say I know, but he was a marvellous Hamlet! That would sort of let actors off. If they'd given a good Iago, they could have raped the dog.'

His mother was happy when Martin, after a wretched time at boarding school, joined the Arts Educational stage school, and soon started getting theatre and television parts. The longest he was ever out of work was eight months and that was before the huge success of *Men Behaving Badly*. But would she have preferred him to be a classical actor like his father? 'No, because I think she was a realist and she could see that I could make a living. And I did *Tartuffe* at the National. She was pleased as punch about that.' But actually HE didn't much enjoy working at the National – he complained afterwards that there was a 'meanness of spirit' about the place – they made him pay to use the car park and didn't even give him a farewell drinks party. And he finds theatre work quite limiting generally. 'You only see other actors, never really mix with the other trades, and the whole day is taken up with looking at your watch.' And he wouldn't do a theatre run at present because 'My daughter's still at home and I don't want to piss that away really.'

He seems very much a settled family man now, but he had quite a wild youth. He says it wasn't THAT wild: 'I went through it all at the appropriate age but not to the degree that people make out. And by the time we made *Men Behaving Badly* it wasn't the appropriate age. That was the joke – that we were too old to be behaving badly. And we were a really hard-working, professional group. That's not to say I never went to a pub with Neil Morrissey, but I wasn't Oliver Reed!' So he didn't have to go into rehab or anything? 'No, because I wasn't ever at a sort of Road to Damascus crisis point. I just grew up.' And then he met Philippa, and had Emily, and moved to the country and 'I felt very happy, and lucky, and that seemed to reflect on what happened to me – I got even luckier, in everything.'

TELL ME, dog-lovers: is it possible to train a dog to demolish a tape recorder? I ask, because after we'd been chatting for about an hour, and Clunes was beginning to show signs of impatience, his big black retriever Arthur stood up and very deliberately wagged his tail over my water glass knocking it on to the tape recorder, which gave a little scream and died. Clunes told me he was sure the tape recorder would recover if I put it in a bag of rice overnight but he seemed quite

64

happy to think the interview was over. But – aha! – I had another tape recorder in my bag and ran to fetch it. However, I do feel that this is where the interview took a turn for the worse.

It started when I quoted a line from the cuttings in which he is supposed to have said that his twenties were 'like one long stag night'. 'I never said that,' he snaps. 'One of your colleagues must have made it up. The press always makes things up. I've got a whole catalogue of things – I've had thirty years of it. When there was talk of us getting back together to make another series of *Men Behaving Badly*, the *Observer* said that we were all going to get paid a quarter of a million to do it – which meant that my tax office looked at my accounts and said, "There's a discrepancy here." Another paper photographed my mother outside her antiques shop so that they could say "Mum behaving badly" – making her cry and cancel going to antiques fairs. And later, when her house was on the market and we knocked fifty grand off the price, the *Sunday Times* added a nought to make it half a million, so they could have the headline "Market behaving badly". But of course when I phoned they said no, no, no, we didn't do it deliberately, it was just a typo. That's pretty hateful, don't you think? Or do you think it's OK?' No, of course I don't think it's OK, I tell him, while privately thinking obviously it must have been a typo.

There is more, much more, a long catalogue of complaints against the press, going back for years. The odd thing is that if you read his cuttings, it is actually very rare to find a negative word against him. But when I suggest that he's had a pretty good press on the whole, he says sourly, 'Apart from them paying money to my ex-wife a couple of times.' I suspect this is the nub. His first wife, Lucy Aston, has twice published kiss' n' tells, brokered, he says, by Max Clifford, describing her life with Clunes as 'all cruelty and cocaine'. She said that he already had a cocaine habit when they married in 1990 but it got steadily worse to the point that he was snorting coke before he set out for work in the mornings. And, perhaps because of the coke, he had a 'mercurial' temper and shouted at her in public. Eventually Lucy booked them in for marriage guidance counselling, but Clunes skipped many of the sessions, or else refused to speak, and soon afterwards left her for Philippa Braithwaite.

As revelations by ex-wives go, the Lucy Aston story wasn't actually in the shock-horror class though I can see it must have made unhappy reading at the time. But if, as he claims, he is always being misquoted, there is one basic precaution he could take, I tell him, which would be to have his own tape recorder on the table. 'That would make for a nice relaxed atmosphere, wouldn't it?' he snorts. 'THAT would be bitter, that would be crazily consumed by it.' But he DOES seem bitter. 'Do you think I'm bitter? I don't think I'm bitter. How should I react to it? Just say oh it's just a bit of fun?'

He is still smiling, while he carries on listing all the crimes journalists have committed – Bernard Ingham said this, Suzanne Moore said that – piling insult after insult on to my profession. There is a truly weird disjunction between his friendly manner and the words coming out of his mouth, so much so that I am genuinely confused about how to react. Eventually when I protest that these are my colleagues he's abusing, he says, all innocent amazement, 'But I'm just telling you what happened.' HE seems surprised that I should object; I am surprised that anyone of any intelligence would decide to vent his hatred of journalists to a journalist. And his anger is all the more chilling for being expressed with a smile.

So why does he give interviews, if he finds them so bruising? 'Publicity,' he says flatly. 'You have to do it for the DVD [series five of *Doc Martin*], it's in your contract.' Would he prefer not to be mentioned in the press at all? 'No I have to be, for what I do. They're complementary industries, aren't they, entertainment and journalism?' Really? How so? 'We go on telly and then you can write about us. And then we're accused of having courted the press.' Right. This is what one might call the Hugh Grant, as opposed to the Marie Colvin, view of journalists – that they exist to serve as minor vassals of the entertainment industry. Unfortunately this belief seems to have become more widespread post-Leveson.

'Well, I'm sorry you've had such a bad time from the press,' I tell him stiffly, gathering up my things to leave. 'It doesn't take up any time in my day,' he assures me. We go into the kitchen while he calls me a taxi, but Philippa appears almost immediately and offers to give me a lift to the station. 'Yes please!' I say eagerly, but he says, 'No, no, the taxi's on its way.' So there is an awkward fifteen minutes when I am stuck in the kitchen with him, longing for my taxi, when he suddenly turns all chummy again, sunshine after rain, and starts raving about *Doc Martin*. 'Eileen is such a hoot,' he says. 'She's absolutely brilliant. And – it sounds a silly thing to say – but so grown-up. Sometimes you wonder what world actors live in, but she mucked in with all the cast and the crew in Port Isaac. All you want is enthusiasm,' he beams. Absolutely, yes, I agree, relieved to see my taxi arriving. I came with absolutely limitless enthusiasm for Martin Clunes and *Doc Martin*. I hope the latter survives.

CHAPTER FIVE

Ethics

I interviewed Martin Clunes when the phone-hacking scandal had just exploded and we journalists were very much on the back foot. He, like Hugh Grant, Steve Coogan and a host of other actors, obviously felt the time was right to clobber the press, even to the point of abolishing its centuries-old freedom. But what shocked me was how many of my friends suddenly started fulminating against journalists. I hadn't realised we were so generally loathed.

Of course, my friends added, 'We don't mean you, Lynn,' but the truth is I am deeply wedded to my profession. I am, and remain, proud to be a journalist, especially in Britain where we have the most varied and lively newspapers in the world (have you ever tried reading the Australian press?) and would be heartbroken if press freedom were abolished. Of course there were abuses, and probably will be again, but they can be curtailed by specific legislation. Most of the outrages that were committed were already illegal anyway.

I have never hacked a phone, or doorstepped a celebrity, but I don't want to sound pi about it because the simple explanation is that I've never worked for the tabloids. And I can't be as disapproving as most of my non-journalist friends seem to be because the fact is: I like *reading* those stories. I do love a big tabloid scandal. I still remember the pleasure I got from Hugh Grant's encounter with a Los Angeles tart, or the Duchess of York's with a fake sheikh. I was really glad to learn that Clint Eastwood's idea of foreplay (according to an ex-girlfriend) was asking, 'Did you floss?' and that Boris Becker managed to father a child in a broom cupboard in Nobu. These sorts of details are the spice of modern life. So, as a reader, I'm complicit in every press intrusion because I enjoy reading the *fruits* of it and would be very sorry if we had the sort of (much stricter) privacy laws they have in France. Incidentally, I'm always shocked that some of my respectable friends who say sniffily that they don't want to know about Hugh Grant's escapades will happily read page after page about gruesome murders and children held captive in cellars – stuff that I find far more troubling and, yes, obscene, than some film star paying for a blowjob.

Because of my weird career trajectory, hopping straight from Oxford to *Penthouse*, and then, after a long career break, to Fleet Street, I never had a proper journalist's training and sometimes wish I had. In particular, I could have done with some training in media law – I had to pick up an understanding of libel as I went along. And it became a very serious matter when I was on the *Sunday Express* in the 1980s because libel damages suddenly shot through the roof – Jeffrey Archer pocketed half a million in 1987 when the *Daily Star* said he'd slept with a prostitute. Consequently, the business of 'legalling' articles – getting them checked and passed by the in-house lawyers – which had been rather a formality before, suddenly became a vital part of my job.

Luckily, we had some excellent in-house lawyers at the *Sunday Express* who took me under their wing and explained that even though I 'felt' that so and so was lying, it wasn't actually advisable to say so in print unless I had some evidence to back it. Eventually we arrived at a good modus operandi whereby, instead of trying to censor myself, I would write whatever I wanted and then send it to the lawyers who would summon me for a sort of viva – a bit like an Oxford tutorial but a lot more fun. They would have my article in front of them with many words underlined and other words crossed out – this was in the days when we still had typewriters and paper, O best beloved, and lawyers had red pens. Then the interrogation would start: What is your evidence for saying this? Are you sure the quote is accurate? Are those his *exact* words? Do you have a shorthand record of it? (Bizarrely, in those days, judges would accept shorthand notes as evidence but not tape recordings – if I ever *had* been sued for libel I would have had to get someone who knew shorthand to make a shorthand transcript of the tape.) These sessions taught me the absolute necessity of keeping tapes, and making sure I transcribed them accurately, and the lesson was duly engraved on my heart.

Then the negotiations would start. 'Do you *have* to describe her hands as "withered"? Couldn't they be weathered?'

'No – they were rather pale.'

'Wrinkled?'

'Well they were wrinkled, but more withered, as if they had shrunk. What about "gnarled"?' I would say, trying to be helpful.

'No, "gnarled" is as bad as "withered". Do you have to describe her hands at all?'

'Yes, because that's the giveaway [we were talking about Zsa Zsa Gabor]. Her face looks pretty good but her hands reveal her age.'

'Oh all right, you can have "withered",' the lawyer would sigh and put a little tick by the word.

Some of the lawyers rather fancied themselves as writers so these discussions could go on, enjoyably, for hours. ' "Poofy", Miss Barber? The *Sunday Express* does not use the word "poofy". Can you suggest an alternative?'

' "Effeminate"?'

'No.'

' "Camp"?'

'I don't think our readers know what that means. "Dandified"?'

'Mm – but that doesn't mean the same as "poofy".'

'Quite.'

Sir John Junor, who had been editing the *Sunday Express* for thirty years when I joined, maintained that you could not be sued for libel if you framed something as a question. It was a practice that seemed to work for him, so I followed it, though I'm not sure it ever had any proper legal basis. Thus, I could ask my old boss Bob Guccione if he was connected with the Mafia, and put the question in the article, so long as I followed it with his denial. But it meant I could at least float the idea, which readers could ponder for themselves. People were terribly shocked in 1990 when I asked Sir Jimmy Savile if it was true that he liked little girls. He had just been given a knighthood! He was a friend of the Royal Family! He had raised zillions for charity! How could I ask him such a terrible thing? But it was a rumour that was very widespread (and subsequently turned out to be true, though not until after his death) and I felt I had to tackle it. Sir Jimmy was momentarily flustered by the question but not, I think, surprised. He obviously knew the rumour existed. And of course he denied it. But at least by posing the question, I'd alerted readers to the possibility.

My sessions with the *Sunday Express* lawyers amounted to a useful libel training, and in fact I only ever landed the paper with one writ – from Frank Warren, the boxing promoter, who was a famously keen litigant – which was settled out of court. But while I was at the *Sunday Express*, I had an extremely lucky libel escape. I was asked to do an article about the fashion world, and happily ran round interviewing designers and attending catwalk shows. I noticed in the latter that Rastafarians seemed to be all the rage – it was a rare show that didn't feature at least one model with dreadlocks. I mentioned this to the fashion editor who said oh yes, Rastafarians were *the* hot new accessory and the designer Katharine Hamnett actually lived with one. I gleefully put this in my article, thinking that the fashion editor's word must be good enough. Alas, it was not (she had mixed Hamnett up with someone else) and we duly received a letter from Hamnett saying that she lived with her husband and didn't even know any Rastafarians. Potentially, she could have sued us for tens of thousands but instead she wrote sweetly that, in case people got the wrong idea, perhaps we could print a small correction? Of course we did, with huge sighs of relief, but it could have been a very costly mistake.

By luck more than judgement, I managed to get through several decades of doing interviews – and often going quite close to the line – without being sued for libel. I ascribe that largely to my habit of tape recording everything and keeping the tapes, but also to discussing potential problems with the in-house lawyers. When I *did* finally find myself in court, in 2011, it was over a book review for the *Telegraph* and I lost. The case took three years to come to court, cost something like £1 million in legal fees (which the *Telegraph* had to pay, thank God, not me) and meant spending literally weeks in consultation with lawyers. My day of cross-examination in court was one of the most unpleasant and exhausting days of my life – the idea that anyone, ever, should 'look forward to their day in court' is insane. The whole process was a nightmare, and I'm very glad it didn't happen to me when I was younger, because it could have permanently shaken my confidence. It must be tempting for young journalists now to avoid all possible legal problems by never writing a single rude word about anyone. But how dull that would be for the readers!

Libel, of course, is the most obvious hurdle you confront as an interviewer, but there are other, much less straightforward ethical questions that have to be decided by your conscience rather than the law. I believe that an article should give an accurate account of what happened in an interview, but some journalists (especially on the *Daily Mail*) don't seem troubled by this rule. They find it alarmingly easy to distort what transpired – for instance, they will give the impression that the interviewee has talked non-stop about their evil ex-husband when in fact they've been trying to plug their pet charity, but have foolishly been lured into uttering a few sentences about their failed marriage, leading to headlines like 'My husband soaked me dry'. I think that's dishonest, but there is no way you could legislate against it. It is up to the individual journalist's conscience.

I remain adamantly opposed to 'copy approval' – the practice of letting interviewees see the article before publication – but it is now routinely demanded by nearly all A-list stars, along with 'photo approval'. I think it is betraying the readers to agree but, as a mere writer, one can only say no – while knowing that some other journalist, probably a freelance, will grab the opportunity. It is up to editors to hold the line but I'm not sure that they can do much longer. 'Copy approval' started creeping in from magazines like *Hello!* in the 1980s but has now spread to other magazines and, I fear, newspapers. It is invidious.

I need to feel, when I go to interview someone, that I am completely free to like them or dislike them and write as I find. But sometimes that freedom can be compromised. Once or twice editors have let me know that the person I'm interviewing is a friend of theirs, or of the proprietor. I try to nip this in the bud by saying, 'So what happens if I can't stand him?' They always say, 'Oh I'm sure you'll love him,' which can sound like an instruction. I remember when I was at the *Telegraph Magazine*, Emma Soames, the then editor, sent me to Los Angeles to interview Michael Chow, the restaurateur. I found him gloomy, oppressive, and his house the same, full of sinister black-lacquer furniture. His much-loved wife Tina Chow had died in tragic circumstances, of Aids. And there was that notorious Helmut Newton photograph of her, in vestal white, being tied up like a roped steer by Michael Chow.

So I gave a pretty sour account of the man. Only then did Emma reveal that he had offered to host a *Telegraph* party at his Mr Chow restaurant in Knightsbridge. But too bad – I couldn't rewrite the piece saying he was all sunshine and light.

Another increasing awkwardness as I get older is that I often have friends in common with the people I am interviewing. The writer India Knight, for instance, is a friend and got me an interview with *her* friend David Baddiel. I'd met him at a couple of her parties and liked him a lot, so I didn't anticipate any problem. And indeed I liked him again when I interviewed him – except that he wanted to talk about a film he'd just made called *The Infidel* which I thought was dire. I put a hint to that effect in my piece, and Baddiel was upset – as he relayed to India. I didn't mind upsetting Baddiel but I did mind upsetting India – though fortunately she was very brisk about it, and told him he couldn't possibly be hurt by one sharp word of criticism – especially as he'd soon be getting hundreds more from real film critics who hated the film as much as I did.

Another problem when you and the interviewee have mutual friends is that you often know things about them that you shouldn't, because you know them from private gossip, not from the press. You might know that A had a hot affair with B last year, but then went back to her husband, or that C's friends are worried about his increasing drug use, or that D has been in therapy for depression. You have to try to banish this knowledge from your mind. But on the other hand, it would be a very unnatural interview for me if I didn't raise topics like fidelity, drugs, depression, so I ask about them but then accept the answers given, even if I know privately that they are untrue. When I interviewed Jeffrey Archer back in the 1980s, I knew that he knew that I knew his mistress, so I felt a bit awkward asking if he believed in marital fidelity. But of course he was the master of the bare-faced lie and able to beam 'Of course' without even the merest tinge of embarrassment.

But this business of background knowledge is always ethically difficult. I prefer 'clean' interviews where I've never met the person before, we have no mutual friends, and all I know about them beforehand is what I've read in the press. Everything has to be found out by questioning, but anything I *do* find is 'mine', legitimately acquired and legitimately published.

The *New Yorker* journalist Janet Malcolm published a book in 1990 called *The Journalist and the Murderer* which people are fond of quoting at me with hostile intent. It starts with the claim: 'Every journalist who is not too stupid or too full of himself to notice what is going on knows that what he does is morally indefensible.' Nothing in the rest of the book substantiates this claim and Malcolm has admitted since that it was 'a piece of rhetoric' but she persists in seeing something morally ambiguous in the writer–subject relationship, namely that it 'seems to depend for its life on a kind of fuzziness, if not utter covertness, of purpose. If everybody put his cards on the table, the game would be over. The journalist must do his work in a kind of deliberately induced state of moral anarchy.' She says that journalists pretend to befriend their subjects and then betray them.

Many journalists worship Janet Malcolm. I don't. She wrote *The Journalist and the Murderer* after she had been caught doctoring quotes in an interview with a psychiatrist to the point of making them mean the opposite of what was said. This would, I'm sure, induce a 'state of moral anarchy' in any journalist – it is axiomatic that you never alter a quote. The other point, though, is that Malcolm does not interview celebrities. Her interviewees tend to be 'real people', whose input she needs in order to construct a bigger story. Her recent *Iphigenia in Forest Hills*, for instance, was about a murder case among the secretive Bukharan-Jewish community in Queens, New York. In order to find out anything at all, presumably she had to befriend her interviewees and some of them might have felt she betrayed them. But she could have argued it was all in the cause of getting inside the community.

However, celebrity interviews are not remotely like that. The participants are old hands at the publicity game, and know that this is a transaction in which we both hope to get something more than we intend to give. The celebrity hopes for maximum publicity for their book or film or whatever they are plugging in return for minimal self-exposure. The journalist delivers the publicity but aims to wrest a few revealing remarks from the celebrity along the way in order to produce an interesting article. Nobody pretends to befriend anyone so there can be no question of betrayal. It is perhaps a somewhat hard-headed transaction, but not, I am sure, a morally ambiguous one. Janet Malcolm is wrong.

CHAPTER SIX

Sportsmen

I've always been reluctant to interview sportsmen, first because I'm not remotely interested in sport and second because sportsmen, whether by temperament or training, never seem to have anything interesting to say. They are not introspective; they are not looking for analysis or validation; they know they can do all their self-expression on the pitch or track or whatever; they regard talking as a very poor substitute for doing. Which is all fair enough. And on a purely professional level, I feel that newspapers devote far too many pages to sport anyway so I don't want to add to them.

While I was at *Penthouse* I moonlighted by doing a series of footballer interviews – one a week – for the *Evening Standard*. The footballers were all the good-looking ones who were thought to appeal to female fans and there was a free poster giveaway with each issue. I was young and pretty then, so perhaps the theory was that I could charm the players into letting their hair down – except that the one time that I did get a footballer (Derek Possee of Millwall) to let his hair down, and talk about all the boozing and partying that went on ('Win or lose, on with the booze'), the editor cut it on the grounds that Millwall's manager would be upset.

While I was at the *Sunday Express* in the 1980s I was sent to interview a famous cricketer called Dennis Lillee, and was handed an envelope to give him. What's in it? I asked (it was strangely thick, as if padded) and my editor rather shamefacedly explained that it was £500. We PAY for interviews? I squawked, shocked to my puritan core. 'Never normally, but you have to with sportsmen,' was the explanation. Lillee gave a stupendously boring interview and in retrospect I wish I'd made some use of the money – I should have waved a tenner at him while asking a question and paid him according to the interest of his answer.

The only remotely interesting sports interview I've ever done is with the tennis player Rafael Nadal when he was at the height of his career. I think of it as my best 'silk purse out of sow's ear' effort – which is a term I often use to myself but perhaps needs explaining. A good interview, I believe, is one in which the subject says so many interesting things that my only problem is deciding which quotes to leave out. Obviously I have to do a certain amount of writing to frame the quotes, but the quotes take precedence. That is, if they're good. A sow's ear, on the other hand, is when the subject has said almost nothing of any interest, and very few of their quotes are usable. It is then up to me to concoct an article, a silk purse, out of thin air. I don't like doing it too often and, as I say, I would always prefer to start from the quotes, but once in a while it allows me to vent my opinions on a wider subject.

With Nadal, it gave me a chance to vent my deep distrust of the whole sports management industry. It is now as tightly controlled as Hollywood in its heyday, or possibly even more so because it is run by a near monopoly, IMG. If a sports writer writes anything disobliging about any of IMG's players, they can have their press passes withdrawn, so they are pretty much forced to be tame. (Actually Nadal left IMG at the end of 2012 to set up his own management company, but IMG still controls most of the other top players.) I often wonder whether sports commentators know a lot more than they're letting on, whether they can see when a player is fixing a match or a game. But of course they could never say it because – quite apart from fear of libel – they would never get a press pass again.

The net result is that it's easier for an outsider like me to barge in and upset the apple cart, as I did with Nadal, than for an insider to tell the truth because it's no skin off my nose if I'm never allowed into a tennis match again. And, actually, I'd be terrified of going to a tennis match again because, judging from the furious emails and tweets I got from Nadal fans, they'd probably lynch me.

From the *Sunday Times*, 5 June 2011

If anyone else tells me what a lovely lad Rafa Nadal is I shall scream. He is not a lad – he has just turned twenty-five, which is admittedly young, but he is in his ninth year on the professional tennis circuit, has won nine Grand Slam titles and is worth at least £68 million. And I didn't find him lovely at all. When I finally met him in his hotel suite in Rome (he was playing the Rome Masters) he was lying on a massage table with his flies undone affording me a good view of his Armani underpants – Armani being one of his many sponsors, natch.

No doubt at this point all his millions of fans will start screaming with envy and resolving to kill me but honestly, kiddos, it was a bit rude. He just lay there glowering at me while I perched awkwardly on a nearby table until eventually his PR, Benito Perez-Barbadillo, fetched me a chair. Benito remained in the background and whenever Rafa didn't like a question (which was pretty much every time I asked one) he asked Benito to 'translate' which meant they conferred in Spanish till the PR delivered some smooth PR-y answer. Nadal's command of English seemed highly variable but never great.

Everyone kept telling me that Rafa was so tired and had had a bad day. But then I was so tired and had had a bad day too, traipsing round the boiling Foro Italico stadium, surviving on bottled water, watching his boring match, waiting for his press conference and then hanging about with mobs of screaming fans waiting for him to emerge from the players' entrance. He eventually came out with a posse of security men, signed a few autographs, had his photo taken with a baby, and was whisked off in his car. I was told to follow and meet him at his hotel, which turned out to be some characterless sports/conference complex miles outside Rome – it could have been in Croydon.

HIS bad day only consisted of playing one short tennis match and signing a few autographs, which I thought was what tennis players were paid to do. He admitted at the press conference that he had played badly, dropping a set to a completely unknown Italian player, but he offered no excuses. However other people were quick to offer them for him: it was the day of Seve Ballesteros' funeral and Rafa was very fond of Ballesteros. When he had to sign his name on the television lens (apparently one of those rituals they do at tennis tournaments) he signed 'Seve' instead of 'Rafa'. And, according to David Law, a radio commentator and media director for Queen's Club who very kindly served as my guide to the tennis world, Rafa was definitely below par the day we met, and two days later was diagnosed with a virus. He then went on to lose the Rome finals to Novak Djokovic, having lost the Madrid Masters to him the Sunday before, so his position as world number one was already beginning to look shaky.

What do we know about Rafa Nadal? Only what his minders want you to. He was born in 1986 in Majorca. His father is a businessman but the whole family is sporty – one uncle was a professional footballer known as the Beast of Barcelona. Another uncle, Toni, a former tennis pro, taught Rafa to play tennis from the age of three, and encouraged him to hold the racquet in his left hand, even though he is naturally right-handed. Rafa played in the Spanish juniors and was urged to go to tennis school in Barcelona but he chose to stay in Majorca with his family – Uncle Toni has been his only coach throughout his career. He started playing professionally when he was just fifteen and won his first Grand Slam at nineteen. He lost his first two Wimbledons but finally won against Roger Federer in 2008. At that point he seemed unstoppable – but then a string of knee injuries (tendonitis) meant he didn't win a title for almost a year and commentators started saying he might have to retire. He missed Wimbledon in 2009 partly because of injury but also because his parents had just split up and he was very upset

– 'For one month I was outside the world.' But he bounced back in 2010 and there has been no talk of tendonitis recently. However, he is now under threat from Djokovic.

Despite his vast wealth – £24 million in winnings, probably twice that in sponsorship – everyone agrees that he is unspoiled, unchanged. His best friends are still the friends he made at school; his hobbies are football, golf and fishing. He goes back to his home town, Manacor, in Majorca whenever he has time, and shares a big apartment block with his mother, sister, grandparents and Uncle Toni and his family. He also has a beach house at Porto Cristo, Majorca (not Ibiza as the press sometimes says) where he likes to go fishing. Two years ago he bought a £2 million beachfront house with its own golf course in the Dominican Republic, but he has never stayed there. I asked if there was some tax reason for choosing the Dominican Republic but he said no – he pays all his taxes in Spain – but he has some property investments in Mexico and thought it would be good to have a base near there for when he retires from tennis. He also has a charitable foundation, run by his mother, which has already opened a school with three tennis courts in India.

Anyway, back to the interview. Since I was perforce staring at his underwear, I decided to ask about it. Frankly, I'm amazed that any underwear company should want to sponsor Nadal, given that his on-court behaviour always screams, 'My pants are killing me!' He can't go five minutes without fiddling with them – they seem to get stuck between his buttocks and then he has to pull them out. I remember the first time I saw him at Wimbledon thinking:

Gosh he's supposed to earn millions – you'd think he could afford some decent underwear by now. Anyway I asked whether his contract stipulated that he should wear Armani underwear on court and he said, 'I don't have to but I am very happy to wear Armani because their underwear is fantastic.' But then why is he always fiddling with it? 'That is something I am doing all my career, something that I cannot control.' Has he ever tried to stop? 'It is difficult for me because it bothers me all the time and I play with different underwears – long, short – but it is impossible to stop.'

Perhaps it's just another of those rituals that all his fans adore. Every time he comes on court, he waves at the crowd, sits down, gets his water bottles out of his bag, takes a sip from each, and then carefully lines them up so that their labels all face precisely the same way. It takes a long time and his opponent is meanwhile standing by the net, waiting for the coin toss, getting quite irritated I imagine. Eventually when Rafa has faffed and fiddled enough, he leaps to his feet and does a sort of Superman swoop across the court and starts jumping up and down in his opponent's face while the umpire tosses his coin. Then he races to the baseline as if he is dying to start the match and his opponent has been cruelly delaying things. The fans love it. What can I say? I asked if he suffered from OCD but of course this required translation and much conferring with his PR and produced the eventual answer, 'It is something that you start to do that is like a routine. When I do these things it means that I am focused, I am competing – it's something I don't NEED to do but when I do it means I am focused.' Does he have other rituals, perhaps in the locker room, before the match? 'I always have a cold shower.' And any particular rituals last thing at night before he goes to sleep? 'No. I have to have the TV or computer on, but I turn it off if I wake up. What I normally do is have dinner, do some work with Rafael my physio, then sleep.' Gripping stuff.

As far as I can see, Nadal has made only one (mildly) controversial remark in his life and that was in 2009 when he criticised Andre Agassi for saying in his autobiography, *Open*, that he had taken crystal meth while he was still on the circuit. Nadal said that tennis was a clean sport, and it was very bad of Agassi to suggest otherwise. Was it really news to him that anyone in tennis took drugs? This requires some heavy conferring with his PR but he eventually comes back: 'Well that's something that's all in the past. But I was shocked. I know Agassi did a lot of good things for tennis but that book wasn't one of those things. You didn't feel bad when you were playing and then you feel bad five years after you retire – it's not a moral thing. Anyway, that is something that is impossible today. We have twenty-five drugs tests a year.' Random ones? 'Sure. A lot of times.'

Agassi also said in his book that he grew to hate tennis, having played it so relentlessly for so long. Nadal says that could never happen to him – he loves tennis – but he wishes the tour could be shorter. All the ATP players have to commit to playing sixteen obligatory tournaments, most of which last two weeks, but Nadal in addition always plays Barcelona, for the sake of his family and Majorcan friends; he also plays Qatar as preparation for the Australian open, and Queen's as preparation for Wimbledon, which means that he plays eleven months a year. And of course, because he is rarely knocked out in the early rounds, he never gets time off. 'For sure,' he sighs, 'the tour is not perfect. In my opinion, three months is the minimum time that you should be off. Because if not, we have a shorter career. Everybody has a shorter career and it's not good for the sport, not good for the players, not good for the fans.' I asked Nadal if his history of knee injuries meant that he would be more crippled at age fifty than someone who had never played tennis, and he said, 'For sure. When you play eleven months of the year, mostly on hard courts, that's what happens, yes.'

So, it's a hard life, and a very very unnatural one. The players live inside a bubble surrounded by these great phalanxes of middle-aged men, big-bellied habitués of the hospitality tent, who don't seem to have anything much to do except talk on their mobiles. If required to do so by a journalist like me, they will effuse about their 'boy' and what a lovely lad he is and how he loves his football and his fishing and is so close to his family, etc etc, wheeling out their tired old stereotype of what a lovely lad consists of, and you think: Hang on, your 'boy' could eat ten of you for breakfast – why do you talk so patronisingly about him? And why do you find it so remarkable that he is still close to his family and that he still sees his old friends? Presumably because you are some multi-divorced adulterous sleazeball who dropped your old friends the minute you moved up in the world. One journalist found it remarkable that Rafa had still not upgraded his mobile phone a year after winning Wimbledon. Rafa (good man) said that it was a perfectly good phone, it worked, why change it? But the journalist seemed to take this as evidence of an almost saintly degree of unworldliness, right up there with the Dalai Lama.

The degree of publicity control in sport is comparable to the heyday of Hollywood, when they had these great studio publicity machines that took young actors as soon as they were signed, and proceeded to invent their life stories for them. Poor Merle Oberon was told she grew up in Tasmania, Australia, when she actually grew up in Bombay, but woe betide any actor who ever deviated from the script. The game was exposed in Oscar Levant's remark, 'I knew Doris Day before she was a virgin,' i.e. before the studio got their mitts on her. And poor old Rock Hudson had to die of Aids before anyone could reveal that he was gay. Incidentally, David Law told me that there are no gays on the tennis tour, which made me boggle a bit.

Anyway it means that sports stars, like Hollywood stars of old, are forced to live within the boring and meagre straitjackets their publicity machines have crafted for them. But once in a while the machine breaks down – most memorably in the case of Tiger Woods. Here was a young man exceptionally good at golf whose minders and sponsors dictated that he was also Mr Wholesome, a clean-living guy devoted to his wife and kids, a role model for would-be golfers – 'lads' – around the world. And lo! he turns out to have a long and sleazy history with hookers. And the world – or at any rate his sponsors – throw up their hands and shout this is APPALLING! We are amazed, we are shocked to the core, we wash our hands of him. Whereas in fact if they were doing their jobs and knew anything at all about him, they would have known, the way studio publicists knew that Rock Hudson was gay, that it was all a charade.

Anyway, I wanted to ask Rafa about Tiger Woods and spent a long time before the interview plotting how I could best raise his name without looking too obvious, but then Rafa saved me the trouble by raising it himself. Almost out of the blue, having talked about Seve Ballesteros (usual paeans), he said, 'But if I have an idol, I love Tiger Woods.' Crikey. I almost fainted with excitement. Er . . . and did his opinion of him change when he found out . . . 'No, it didn't change my opinion of him because I don't care about his personal life. Nobody must care about his personal life – Tiger Woods is a very important person in the world because he plays golf.' But when he's been marketed as this great clean-living role model for the young and then it turns out . . .? 'Well I don't want to discuss about these things but in my opinion' – which unfortunately requires a great deal of translation and discussion with his PR who eventually comes back with: 'He says that Tiger never hurt anybody in the outside world, he only hurt himself. He is a role model for him on the golf course and also in public because he always behaved properly. But what he does in private is his personal life, nobody else's, and Rafa says his problems with his wife are HIS problems with HIS wife, not anybody else's.' Yes, but there's a certain hypocrisy when he's been marketed as Mr Clean? This question doesn't seem to need translation because Rafa responds sharply, 'Well. Anyway. Next question.'

Right. Which brings me to the subject of The Girlfriend. Her existence was first unveiled to the world by Uncle Toni in 2008 (though unveiled is perhaps not the word) when he said that Rafa had a childhood sweetheart back home in Majorca called Maria Francisca Perello, or Xisca for short. Rafa was quoted as saying, 'She is perfect for me, because she is very relaxed and easy-going and I've known her for a long, long time. Our families have been friends for many years.' Hardly the language of passion you'll agree but at least from then on he had an official Girlfriend, which made up for the fact that his sleeveless tops and bulging biceps reminded one inexorably of Freddie Mercury.

But The Girlfriend remains a distant presence, never actually around. She sometimes make an appearance at his finals, among his family, but even long-time tennis insiders like David Law have never met her. Rafa says that he sees her whenever he goes back to Majorca but that is only maybe thirty days a year. For a young man in peak physical condition, it doesn't suggest the height of sexual fulfilment.

Anyway I asked if he was going to marry The Girlfriend and he said flatly, 'No.'

Me: No??!!??!!

'Not now, no. I don't have any plans in that way.'

'Do you mean you've split up?'

'No. I don't talk about the girlfriend in public, but I have the same girlfriend since many years.'

'When do you meet?'

'Her house is very close to my house so when I am in Majorca I see her, and when she has holidays sometimes she comes to the tournaments, but she cannot follow the tour around because she has to do her work. [She works for a big insurance company.] She has her life and I have my life.'

'Do you think she'll wait for you? To get married when you finish tennis?'

'I didn't ask her to.'

'But if you only see her – what? – thirty days a year, it can't be a very fulfilling relationship?'

Rafa for the first time in our interview seems to turn his full attention on me, a laser stare, and for a second I can imagine what it must be like to stand on the baseline waiting to receive his serve. 'But do you care about my relationship?' Well no, I have to admit, as the ace whizzes past me, of course I don't really care about his relationship, I'm just doing my job. Somehow this breaks the tension, and we both laugh.

Rafa: I understand your point, but I never talk about my girlfriend. I have a fantastic relationship with her, we understand each other. It is not a problem for her if I travel every week and for me not a problem if when I am in Majorca she has to work all day.

Me: Do you talk on the phone though?

Rafa: No. When I am in a tournament I have to concentrate. Sure, I talk every day with her.

Me: I'm confused now.

Rafa: Forget about my girlfriend.

Me: Do you phone your mother every day?

Rafa: Yes. My mother, my sister, my father, everybody.

I AM confused. I can only record that there was a big difference in the enthusiasm with which he said he phoned his mother and sister every day, and whatever he was saying, or not saying, about his girlfriend. According to the Majorcan press, they split up last year, but then got together again.

91

Before that there were rumours that he was 'close' to the Danish player Caroline Wozniacki. There was also a curious episode a year and a half ago when he made a 'steamy' video with the Colombian singer Shakira for her single 'Gypsy' and was photographed having what seemed like a romantic dinner with her. It looked like an attempt to rebrand him as a stud. But his PR later revealed that he was present, along with Rafa's manager, Shakira's manager and other members of their respective teams, so it was hardly a tête-à-tête. And Rafa says he has 'no plans' to do more videos with Shakira, or with any other pop singers.

Listen: I dare say Rafael Nadal really is a lovely man (though I refuse to say 'lad'). But the point I'm trying to make is that whether he is or isn't I wouldn't know, and you wouldn't either. He lives within this tight stockade of team Rafa, and sticks to the script his minders have written for him. It must require great discipline to be so controlled, but then it must require great discipline to be a world champion anyway. Oh for a McEnroe, a Connors, an Agassi! There was a time, O best beloved, when tennis players had tempera-ments, when they threw racquets and shouted at umpires and had sex in broom cupboards and often behaved quite badly. Nadal has never thrown a racquet in his life – his Uncle Toni trained him not to. And the tennis player HE most admires is Björn Borg, whom he admires precisely because he had 'ice in his veins' – which was what always made him so deadly dull to watch. But Borg, we might note, retired at twenty-six, not from injury but because he was burned out. All that discipline must take its toll on a young man. Even more than the injuries, the psychological attrition of having to be on your best behaviour every day, to play match after match, to give press conference after press conference, to meet and greet sponsors, the sheer boredom of living on this treadmill, must wear anyone down. And for Nadal already the best may be over. He was number one when I started this article, but will probably be number two by the time you read it. I asked if he might retire at twenty-six, as Borg did. 'If I have injury I could. You never know. But it's something I prefer to believe is not going to happen.' How will he know when to retire? 'When I don't have enough motivation to go on court and play every day and love the competition. But that is not the case at the moment.'

Do you think physical or psychological wear and tear will make you stop eventually? 'I really don't know. Nobody knows the future. I don't know if I will be injured before mentally, or physically. It is something you cannot plan.'

*

I'd only recently joined Twitter when I published this piece, and it gave me my first experience of being trolled. Every Nadal fan in the world, it seemed, wanted to tell me they hoped I got cancer. It was upsetting of course – on the other hand, it left me with twice as many Twitter followers as I'd had before. Some of them stopped following me after the frenzy died down, but most of them stayed. Since then, I've learned that you can always boost your Twitter following by writing something rude – it seems that the people who follow you in order to abuse you are just as loyal as the ones who like you. And among the torrents of abuse, I did have one or two sober messages of support, as well as the priceless photographs of 'Capybaras who look like Rafael Nadal' which you can still find online.

CHAPTER SEVEN

In Extremis

I said that writing up my interview with Rafa Nadal felt like making a silk purse out of a sow's ear. This one with Christopher Hitchens shortly before he died was the complete opposite: I was given a silk purse and my only problem was not ruining it. The responsibility was all the greater because we both knew that he was dying.

I had interviewed him once before in 2002, for the *Observer*, over a typically boozy five-hour lunch. (I could barely walk when we left, but he was still going strong, in fact went straight on to speak in an Orange Word debate.) I avoided asking much about his politics but instead asked about his mother's death – it was not a subject he had talked about before, though he did later in his autobiography – and he seemed to welcome this unusual foray into personal reminiscence. He was pleased with the article and was always friendly when we ran into each other subsequently at *Private Eye* lunches or at the Hay Festival.

Then came the news that he had inoperable cancer, which he wrote about in *Vanity Fair*. It sounded as though he was pretty near the end. But in January 2011, Sarah Baxter, the editor of the *Sunday Times Magazine*, said, 'Christopher Hitchens wants you to interview him – but he's in Washington.

What do you feel?' What did I feel? I didn't hesitate: I felt that a summons from Hitchens was one I could not refuse.

It was then almost a decade since I'd flown to the States; I had developed a real phobia about it, ever since I had a panic attack in the New York immigration hall. So when I joined the *Sunday Times* in 2009, I made it a condition that I would never have to fly to the States – I didn't mind flying to Europe, but never to the States. Sarah Baxter was surprised (editors generally love flying) but accepted it. But then when she said Christopher Hitchens wanted to see me in Washington, I positively leapt on the plane. And I am so glad I went.

From the *Sunday Times*, 4 March 2011

Reading the Prologue to Christopher Hitchens' autobiography *Hitch-22* is a spooky experience now because it seems to say so clearly that he knows he is dying. It is even called 'Prologue with Premonitions' and starts with him reading a magazine article that refers to 'the late Christopher Hitchens'. I was sent an early copy of the book and thought as soon as I read it that he must have been diagnosed with some terminal illness. But in fact he hadn't. He wrote the Prologue in late 2008 – the news that he had inoperable cancer came in June 2010 when he was just starting the publicity tour for the book. To anyone who asked the prognosis, he said, 'I have inoperable metastasised stage four oesophagal cancer – and there is no stage five.' He seemed to accept that he was on the way out.

But things have changed a bit since then, and are still changing all the time. Long bouts of heavy chemo eradicated most of the nodes round his collarbone, though there is one that stubbornly remains. The big fear is that the cancer will spread to his liver and it is well placed to do so. But the chemo is over now and his hair is growing back. When he did his television debate with Tony Blair in Toronto last November he looked almost like the Dalai Lama – bald as an egg, plump and benign. This was the Hitch I was expecting to meet. But this time at home in Washington he looks different again – his cheeks are covered with grey stubble but he is painfully thin. Oddly, the effect is to make him look Jewish – which he likes. He was pleased to discover, long after his mother's suicide, that she was Jewish – she had kept the secret to her grave.

He looks much sterner than usual, but greets me as an old friend. 'It's very nice to see you again. I glimpsed you at the Hay Festival, I think?' Ah – I was hoping he hadn't seen me – I avoided him because I had just published a negative review of his book. 'Oh it wasn't too bad,' he laughs. 'Anyway I don't brood on reviews any more. It's sad that a nice one no longer makes my day, but a bad one no longer wrecks it.'

He shows me round the apartment, which is vast – acres of parquet floors, a grand piano, miles of bookshelves, paintings stacked against the walls. It's a long way from Martin Amis's 'sock'. And barely have I finished admiring the rolling vistas, when he says, 'But you will want to smoke? We'd better go next door,' and takes me to the next-door apartment which is only marginally smaller. He says he bought it years ago, for storage, but recently started doing it up, until his illness intervened. It is now reserved for smoking, the main apartment being kept smoke-free for the sake of his daughter, Antonia, seventeen. We sit at the kitchen table, he pours me a glass of red wine and himself a whisky, and settles down to talk.

So. How does he feel? 'Today I feel . . . normal. I hope it will be true tomorrow too. But I don't really know till I wake up every day. Some days this terrible lassitude, chronic fatigue, comes and nothing can be done. But I'm not puking any more for example, which was the worst thing – and I had months of that. I can eat again.' They had to stop the chemo, he explains, because his bone marrow packed up and also his gall bladder, which they removed. And anyway by then he had 'junkie arms' from all the needles, and they could no longer find a vein. So now he is on a different treatment, just a pill, which might or might not work.

Is he still writing 1,000 words a day? 'No. Can't do that. There are days when I can only really read.' However, he has been delivering his *Vanity Fair* column every month, and also regular book reviews for *Atlantic Monthly* and odd pieces for *Slate*. And he is thinking of doing a short book on what he calls 'The Malady'. He was wary of writing about his cancer at first – 'I wanted to be very careful to avoid a certain kind of sentimentality' – but Graydon Carter, the editor of *Vanity Fair*, pressed him and he found that, 'at least to begin with, it was quite easy. I didn't exactly think: Whoopee, I've got a whole new subject! But there seems no point in NOT writing about it. And so I have done, and will do, if I am spared.'

The interesting thing, he says, is that his cancer has given him entrée into a whole new world of experimental medicine, thanks to Francis Collins. Collins is not only a top scientist – he ran the human genome project – but also a leading evangelical Christian and Hitch did some debates with him when he published his book *God Is Not Great*. 'He contacted me when I got ill and said, "Is there anything I can do?" And I'm now one of the very few people who've had their whole genome sequenced. And just last month, they told me that they'd found a little mutation and there is a medicine – a very rare and rather expensive medicine – designed for this mutation, which I am now taking. I've been on it for two or three weeks and I will soon find out if it works.'

Do any of his doctors hold out hope of a cure? 'The word cure has not been used, no. But they can maybe keep me alive till better treatments come along. When they run tests on my heart, my liver, my blood pressure, they all come out very strong for someone of my age [sixty-one], and they say if we can keep you going, there are things we might be able to try really quite soon. So that's the way I'm living now. It's a bit vertiginous, but it's not dull!'

Enter Carol Blue, his wife, a dramatic figure with a wonderfully gravelly voice, a huge mane of black hair, pencil-thin black trousers and fuck-me shoes. She is apt, I learn later, to refer to herself as a 'broad' and it seems appropriate. She wants to know if she should order a Chinese takeaway for supper. Yes, says Hitch, reeling off an enormous list of food, after checking that I will pay. She disappears to phone the restaurant.

But, I go on, it's so extraordinary that he wrote that Prologue as if he knew he was dying. He must have had SOME inkling? 'No. I constantly got clean bills from the quack

– rather undeservedly, given that I don't take much exercise . . .' [I can't suppress a snort at this point – lack of exercise is hardly the most obvious of his damaging habits.] But I did realise that I was getting tired very easily. I remember when they showed me the schedule of my book tour, thinking quite calmly: I won't get to the end of that.' He also remembers that when he drove past Tintern Abbey on his way to Hay last summer, 'I had this thought that I was looking at it for the last time. So I think with a part of myself I may have known I was wasting.'

He was just embarking on the American leg of his book tour when he collapsed. He woke in his New York hotel room and thought he was having a heart attack – he couldn't breathe – and summoned an ambulance. He had a busy day coming up – an appearance on the Jon Stewart show, a debate with Salman Rushdie at the New York Y, and also a debate with his brother Peter Hitchens about Peter's book, *In Defence of God*. Carol was flying up from Washington to attend these events, but when she phoned the hotel, they said Hitch had gone.

The hospital quickly diagnosed the immediate problem as fluid round his heart, which they drained, and discharged him. But they also said he should make an urgent appointment to see an oncologist – the first hint that he might have cancer. Meanwhile he trotted off to fulfil his speaking engagements. Carol eventually found him standing outside the back entrance of the Y Theatre having a cigarette with his agent. She recalls, 'We saw each other from two blocks away and I went running towards him, I was just so happy to see him! And then we went through the whole night, smiling and socialising as if nothing was wrong. But I remember I was seeing him for the first time as someone who was under a big shadow.'

Next day Hitch made an appointment with an oncologist, had a biopsy, and then carried on with his book tour while waiting for the results. But then he collapsed again at Boston Airport, on the way to giving a talk at Harvard, and was taken to hospital where they finally delivered the verdict – stage four oesophagal cancer. 'I asked if I was going to die, and they said no, not immediately. But one of them said you've got a year. And you don't forget the first time you're told that.' His publishers issued a press statement cancelling his book tour, and explaining why.

The chemo was exhausting, but in breaks between sessions he was able to keep some of his speaking engagements – including the Toronto debate with Tony Blair on 'Is religion a force for good in the world?' He was feeling very ill on the day and worried that he would be sick on stage, but he wasn't, and easily won the debate against an unusually nervous Blair.

But then there was a crisis at New Year when Hitch very nearly died. He'd spent Christmas with Carol's parents in California (her father is a theoretical scientist at Stanford) but was feeling 'beyond exhausted' and was taking enormous quantities of painkillers for a terrible pain in his abdomen. Eventually he was rushed to hospital, 'And I could tell from the expressions on their faces that they were very frightened – my normally unflappable oncologist exclaimed to Carol, "He's crashing!" What had happened was my bone marrow had gone south and both the red and white cells had collapsed at the same time and my gall bladder had gone rancid. But they got me just in time, gave me a huge blood transfusion, and took out the gall bladder. That was what you might call a dress rehearsal, very unpleasant.'

The worst thing now, he says, is being housebound by fatigue. He used to travel three or four times a month and made a point of going at least once a year to countries in turmoil – normally he would have been on the first plane to Tunisia, Egypt, Libya. But now he barely leaves the apartment. 'Just going down to the bank is becoming an adventure.'

Why was he always so eager to fly into dangerous situations? Was it to show he was a tough guy, to prove his physical courage? Partly, he admits, it might have started as a need to impress his father, 'the Commander', who was a genuine war hero. But mainly just, 'The flight from ennui. I hate being bored. I'd rather go to a collapsing country than just sit around. But also I think it's a responsibility to go out and see what is happening elsewhere, to be an internationalist.' Still, it leaves him open to the charge of revolutionary tourism. 'Sure. And voyeurism. One is aware of that. But it's better than not going at all.'

Carol returns with mountains of Chinese food and we move to the dining room. Hitch falls on the food and starts guzzling. 'It's like having a teenage bulimic in the house,' she growls. I ask how they met, and he recalls that it was at the United Airlines baggage reclaim at LA Airport in 1989. He was doing his first ever book tour and his publishers said they could afford to fly him to LA but they couldn't afford a hotel, but they knew this girl, Carol Blue, who worked at the *LA*

Times and liked having writers to stay. Hitch: 'I'd left a message saying that she should look for an Englishman who was past his best and when she arrived I thought: Well I bet it's not her, but she came towards me . . .' Carol: 'He went on and on about being past his best – he was only thirty-nine years old. And then he took me to Romania – he was so clever – just as Ceauşescu was being shot, and it was really wonderful, because it was like being in a scene from *Potemkin* or something . . .' Hitch tries to interrupt – he can see me thinking revolutionary tourist – but Carol is unstoppable. 'There was all this sniper fire and we were in the back of a pickup truck, and we'd been given stacks of newspapers with the headline "Ceauşescu Killed", and there were peasants cheering us on and we were throwing the newspapers off the truck and it was extraordinary – we were bringing the news of the revolution. We saw dead soldiers on the road and we ended up touring the morgue.' And this was like their honeymoon? 'Exactly! I found it FASCINATING. I'd studied political theory and I felt I was finally experiencing a key moment in history.' Hitch emails me afterwards to say it wasn't actually their honeymoon but it was the first time they'd travelled together, and, 'The timing was perfect in that Ceauşescu was killed that week. Whenever I see (or, now, read about) moments of liberation, I always find myself thinking: What a great time this would be to be in love!'

Given that Carol is a considerable character in her own right, I find it astonishing that Hitch barely mentions her in his autobiography, nor his first wife Eleni Meleagrou, nor his three children, Alexander and Sophia by his first marriage, and Antonia. The omission is all the more marked because he gushes away about his male friends, Martin Amis, James Fenton, Ian McEwan, Salman Rushdie, like any besotted lover, but wives and children don't get a look-in. He says I was not the only reviewer to complain about this – 'I began to think there must be some reviewers' central committee that said you have to keep saying he should have written a different book, about his wives.'

So why didn't he? 'If you do it properly, you have to do it at considerable length, and the book was already much too long. And – I suppose I have to say this but I don't know how it will sound – if you do it for one, you have to do it for all. I mean I've been married more than once and there were girlfriends before and I know from friends that it's a very easy way of creating a huge pile of bad blood. So I decided not to do it at all. I don't mention Anna Wintour's name, for example, though my publishers wanted me to. [He went out with her in the mid 1970s, when she was fashion editor of *Viva*, owned by my old boss Bob Guccione, in New York.] She's contacted me I forget how many times, asking me not to cooperate with unauthorised biographies or profiles of her, to the point where I'm not mentioned in her unauthorised biography at all. Anyway, this has gone too far . . .'

How many Anna Wintours might there be? 'Oh I wouldn't like to say, but enough to get in the way of what I wanted the book to be about.' Couldn't he have omitted the girlfriends but written something about his wives and children? 'You don't know these women! No, not to go near it, just to stay completely clear of it. I don't want to read it from other people, and I don't want to do it myself.' Carol says she's fine with it. As for the children, he says they don't read his stuff anyway.

He has finished making his will, and appointed his agent, Steve Wasserman, as his literary executor. But unfortunately, he has no great literary archive to leave – no manuscripts, no letters from Amis and Rushdie and Fenton – because he always throws everything away. 'What I've got,' he says, 'wouldn't fill a box.' But luckily he has still got – because Carol kept it – the very nice letter he received from George W. Bush after he'd talked about his cancer on television. She digs it out for me – handwritten, in a hard-backed envelope, embossed with a presidential seal. 'Thank you for sharing your battle with cancer in that remarkable interview. There's no telling how many folks you will inspire whether you think it works or not. I truly will pray for you. Fight on. You contribute meaningfully to our country's discourse. God bless.' As Carol says, it's not very exciting, but it's not illiterate either, and Hitch was pleased to get it. He got hundreds of letters in the first few weeks after his diagnosis, from famous people and strangers, and still gets three or four a week.

I wondered if he'd had any letters from people he'd fallen out with, but he said no. 'I can't say there's been any sort of moist reconciliations. Sidney Blumenthal has not written but in a sense I don't mind; I think he feels wronged by me and I think he'd feel a hypocrite writing. I did actually write to him when he got stomach cancer but for all I know that only irritated him.' He fell out with Blumenthal in 1999 when Blumenthal, who worked at the White House, testified that he had not been spreading smears about Monica

Lewinsky and Hitch said oh yes he had, and offered to give evidence that could potentially have put Blumenthal in jail for perjury. Several of their mutual friends have not spoken to Hitch since.

What about his brother, Peter – any *rapprochement* there? 'Well there's nothing much to *rapproche*. We're very different types and we've never been close. If it wasn't for our political coloration, no one would be interested.' For decades, Peter tub-thumped for the Right, Hitch for the Left, but Hitch of course has moved rightwards and their main area of disagreement now is God. Does he know whether Peter is praying for him? 'He's had the decency not to say so, but I suppose he is. It's some kind of obligation, isn't it? But he did something very nice which hadn't occurred to me: he said if I needed a bone marrow transplant, he would be happy to give it. Which I thought was very good of him.'

After demolishing the Chinese supper, Hitch announces that next day we are invited to lunch with the British Ambassador. Is that normal? I ask. 'Oh yes, I'm forever rubbing shoulders with the quality!' he laughs. What about the White House? Does he get asked to lunch there? No, he says sorrowfully – he once gave a lecture at the White House (and had his shoes shined for the occasion) but he has never met Obama, though he voted for him. 'It's annoying. It's like living in Washington and not going to see the Lincoln Memorial.'

The funny thing is that we British journalists still think of Hitch as one of our own – but he has lived in the States for over thirty years and became an American citizen in 2007. He no longer follows British politics and says he doesn't recognise half the names in *Private Eye* – he doesn't know who Ed Balls is for example. But his fondness for England is still strong. When his appetite returned after the chemo, he asked for Marmite and Oxford marmalade and Branston pickle, and told Jeremy Paxman to bring him the memoirs of George MacDonald Fraser. One of Hitch's great fears is that he might never see England again. He wants to revisit not just his usual haunts – London and Oxford and Hay – but Dartmoor and Cornwall and parts of Sussex where he grew up. Carol says eagerly, 'Could we go in the spring?' but he makes no promise.

Next day I go to collect them for the Ambassador's lunch. Hitch has clearly made an effort – he is newly shaved, and wearing a blazer. Carol is still getting dressed – he complains that she has a horror of being early, he of being late – but eventually emerges in stilettos and jeans, plus a huge fur hat and a jacket with a gap at the back to show her thong. While we are waiting for a taxi, I ask if she will tell me her age but she says, 'Nah. Why should I? Some of my greatest chums, like Melina Mercouri, would never tell their age. You can say early fifties if you must.'

As soon as we arrive at the Residence, Hitch starts shimmering like Stephen Fry, greeting the butler by name, asking for his 'usual' (whisky) and smoothly introducing me to Sir Nigel and Lady Sheinwald. We are only five for lunch, but it is formally served, with footmen and printed menu cards. Hitch had warned me beforehand that our conversation must be strictly off the record. It was unfortunate to say the least, therefore, that while they were all chatting away about plays they had seen, my handbag suddenly started chatting loudly too. In all my years using tape recorders, this has never happened before – the bugger somehow managed to turn itself on and launch itself into replay at full volume – and there were an embarrassing few minutes while I violently attacked my handbag and the Ambassador stared.

Afterwards we went back to the apartment for Hitch to be photographed and Carol talked movingly about how good he has been throughout his illness. 'He has been without any self-pity, any despondency, but just absolute realism, and almost a kind of poetry in explaining his condition. And he'd get up and try and write and hold conversations – imagine having the worst flu you've ever had and getting up every day. And our dinner table when people came round – I mean Hitch at his illest is still a scintillating conversationalist.'

He is indeed. I was expecting to find him stoical, but what impressed me even more was the sort of gallant bravado he brings to his situation. Why does he feel he needs to fly into collapsing countries to prove his courage? He is proving it now, every day. Only once, in all our conversation, did he seem near tears. He told me that he thought his right vocal cord had gone and, 'If I did lose my voice I would feel that that was . . . No, actually, I can't bear to think about that. That would give me depression which I have not yet had.

'But if I were ever threatened with morose moments, the thing that would cheer me up is that some people who I admire for being very courageous and for having helped free their countries still keep in touch. This is my answer to your question about revolutionary tourism – I didn't just do it for that reason but to try and clarify the situation. And it does make me proud, the friendship with those people who I knew when they were dissidents.'

*

He died on 16 December 2011 – having lived a few months longer than his doctors predicted. The obituaries were wonderful, full of real love as well as appreciation. Ian McEwan's description of their last days together at his cancer clinic in Houston was particularly moving – Hitch insisting on being helped (with all his drips) to his desk and writing an essay on G.K. Chesterton he had promised.

But the BBC *Today* programme struck a sour note when it described him as 'a journalist, an atheist and an alcoholic'. Hitch used to get furious if people called him an alcoholic and I remember this was an issue when I first interviewed him for the *Observer*. I saw him, over lunch, drink three or four whiskies and at least one bottle of wine but he insisted that he had never missed a deadline, never slurred his speech, never at any point been incapable and therefore could not be an alcoholic. Kingsley Amis used to make the same argument, equally unconvincingly. But of course the definition of an alcoholic is infinitely flexible – Californians consider anyone who drinks more than one glass of wine an alcoholic. I remember once interviewing the actress Ali MacGraw who talked at length about how she'd been in rehab and was now a 'recovering alcoholic' and had turned her life around. How much were you drinking at your peak? I asked. 'One evening I drank a whole bottle of red wine!' she confessed wide-eyed. It was all I could do not to guffaw.

The most jarring reaction to Hitch's death came from my

younger daughter. I was raving on about how brilliant and witty he was and what a loss to journalism, and asked if she'd ever read any of his articles. She said no – but she thought he was brilliant on *I'm a Celebrity . . . Get Me Out of Here!*. Hitch on *I'm a Celeb*? It was one of those moments when the earth tilts on its axis. It took quite a lot of hard interrogation to establish that she meant the actor Christopher Biggins, and I wondered, not for the first time, how I could have so failed to educate my daughters.

CHAPTER EIGHT

Pop Stars

I love, love, *love* interviewing pop stars – I wish I'd done more of them. Obviously I mean the ones who write their own stuff and are mad as snakes – I'm not keen on squeaky-clean members of manufactured boy bands who do what Simon Cowell tells them. The ones I admire are those who started writing and composing in their teens, pouring their hearts out alone in their bedrooms, often with no encouragement at all. And who then had the guts to go out and expose themselves to the ridicule of their schoolmates by getting up on stage. So brave, so young! I think they're heroic.

I was lucky in that I just caught on to pop music at the last minute, when so many of my contemporaries missed it. Pop music while I was growing up in the 1950s was terrible, you have no idea. At school, we listened to the Top Ten where the choice was between Liberace, Lonnie Donegan, ghastly Bill Haley, and soppy Paul Anka. (I know there were great people like Chuck Berry and Little Richard performing in the States, but we never heard of them at Lady Eleanor Holles School.) Consequently my friends and I preferred trad jazz and took the ferry over to Eel Pie Island every Saturday to listen to Acker Bilk. What is maddening in retrospect is that we could have been taking the bus to the Station Hotel in Richmond, a couple of miles down the road, to listen to the nascent Rolling Stones, but, again, we'd never heard of them.

So, aged sixteen, I believed that pop music was rubbish and trad jazz was what you had to listen to if you aspired to be a beatnik which I did. And then the situation got complicated because my much older conman boyfriend introduced me to classical music and I realised I had an awful lot to catch up on. I think this is what happened to most of my contemporaries – they graduated very quickly from pop to jazz to classical music and never went back. Luckily, I did.

What saved me was that a friend of mine called Lizzie had a younger sister who, for some reason that I still don't understand, 'discovered' the Beatles before most of the world had heard of them – i.e. in 1962 rather than 1963. Lizzie's sister's bedroom was entirely covered with posters of the Beatles and she played 'Love Me Do' on her Dansette all day long. Of course she was younger than us so we pretended to despise her tastes and asked patronisingly how her 'insects' were coming along, but it meant that when the Beatles did finally arrive, with *Please Please Me* in 1963, I already felt I owned them. And, like anyone who followed the Beatles' career from start to finish, I learned through them to take pop music seriously.

Unfortunately being so keen on the Beatles meant I missed out on many of the other great pop groups who emerged in the 1960s – there were just so many of them! I saw the Animals at an Oxford commem ball but I never saw the Kinks or the Small Faces and I stupidly still ignored the

Rolling Stones till years later. (Mick Jagger is second top – Rupert Murdoch is first – on my perennial wish list of people I want to interview, though he is well known to be a useless interviewee – he claims not to remember the past.) And I missed nearly all the pop stars who emerged in the 1970s because I was deep in nappies. David Bowie still remains a complete blank.

But I did catch up with some of them later, interviewing Rod Stewart, Boy George, Morrissey, long after their peaks. Morrissey was a weird one. I interviewed him in 2002 when he was touring the States, trying to establish a solo career but without much success, and I met him in a most unlikely army town called Colorado Springs where I would have thought they shot people like Morrissey on sight. He was staying at a sort of golf-spa hotel a few miles out of town, and cut a lonely, miserable figure. He was obsessed at the time with a lawsuit brought by one of his former bandmates, and he was so busy telling me chapter and verse of this lawsuit I could hardly get him to talk about music at all. I got the impression his career was washed up but (as so often) I was wrong.

I also had a very funny experience in the 1980s, watching a group called Tears for Fears shoot a video in the California desert. Actually I should call them 'Tear for Fear' because only one of them, Curt Smith, was present – the other one didn't like flying. Curt had to ride around on a quad bike lip-synching 'Everybody Wants To Rule The World'. I and a couple of other journalists were meant to follow around in a Winnebago caravan, together with the PR, Mariella Frostrup. I must say that much as I admire Mariella's subsequent career on radio and television, I have never admired her as much as I did then. We journalists were all jet-lagged and grumbling, the driver kept getting lost, the Winnebago developed engine trouble, the temperature was in the high thirties, we seldom if ever caught up with Tear for Fear but Mariella bubbled on. We were running so late that we didn't arrive at our final location till after midnight. It was by a lake, called Salton Sea, but because it was dark we couldn't see it. My God, we could smell it though – an extraordinary smell which was revealed in the morning to come from heaps of rotting fish all round the lake shore. Mariella kept exclaiming, 'Isn't it picturesque!' But it was hard even to see, our eyes were streaming so badly from the poisonous fumes.

I suppose my favourite pop star ever was Jarvis Cocker, whom I first interviewed in 1998. But for some bizarre reason, he insisted on doing the interview at my house. This caused me a sort of category confusion – I found it hard to be an interviewer and a hostess at the same time – and also I was star-struck which is a terrible fault in an interviewer. Before he came, I spent hours whirling round the house, hiding the more embarrassing family photos, trying to arrange my CDs in some sort of faintly plausible order, banishing the pot-pourri (he once described pot-pourri, along with Belgian chocolates, as his 'worst fear') and generally behaving like a demented fan. Of course I *am* a fan (Pulp's 'Common People' is my favourite pop song ever) but you can't be a fan while doing an interview because you have to try to meet as equals. Years later I interviewed Jarvis Cocker again, at *his* home in Paris, and we had to make lunch for his stepson and again there was this confusion between the domestic and the professional, between him cooking fish fingers and me laying the table while asking questions. I think Jarvis does it deliberately as a way of 'keeping things real', which I approve of in theory but in practice find difficult. Perhaps I don't really want interviews to be too 'real' – I need my professional armour.

Recently, I went to Paris to interview a pop star again, this time Pete Doherty of the Libertines and Babyshambles. It was in a strange, scuzzy, evil-smelling flat with piles of books on the floor and a big shaggy dog sniffling around, but it turned out the flat was not his own but a friend's so whatever clues it might have yielded were misleading. I told myself beforehand not to let myself be charmed by Doherty – of course he charmed me within minutes, not least by saying, 'Are you *really* Lynn Barber? I'm so honoured.' He is, or seems to be, a very sweet lost soul. But I find drug-users very difficult to understand. Barely ever having taken drugs myself, I can never tell if they are 'on' something and how far gone they might be. Doherty at one point used a menthol inhaler and I got wildly excited thinking this must be some new way of snorting cocaine. Doherty mischievously urged me to try it – it had no effect at all, apart from clearing my sinuses. Doherty told me he was off heroin – but he told another interviewer, just a few days later, that he was on a maintenance dose. Who knows? I feel I am too old, now, ever to understand drug-users.

Drunks, of course, are a different matter. My father and plenty of my friends are or were big drinkers and I am not exactly teetotal myself so I don't feel fazed by interviewing alcoholics. But this one, below, with Shane MacGowan, was a marathon, and one that came back to haunt me when my husband died.

From the *Observer*, 11 March 2001

Five o'clock, Bloom's Hotel, Dublin. Shane MacGowan tumbles out of the lift into my waiting arms. The photographer and his assistant and I have been waiting since three, with a cheery Irish PR saying, 'Oh, this is nothing – he kept a journalist waiting four hours yesterday!' I want to murder him. We made various sorties to Shane's hotel room but were blocked by a burly man who seemed to be acting as his minder.

So on the one hand I am relieved to see Shane at last. On the other hand, I quite want to bundle him back in the lift and forget him. I was prepared for the teeth, the famous blackened stumps, but the suit is an unanticipated horror show, with its thickening patina of stains down the trousers culminating in big blobby spatters on the shoes. If he has not been sick down his trousers several dozen times, he must have a very good stylist. His skin has the shiny pallor of someone who has never seen daylight. He lurches towards the bar. The photographer tries to head him off, saying he wants to do photographs outside before the daylight fades. Shane says, 'Ginantonic' and plonks himself in a chair. I chatter brightly about James Joyce; Shane mumbles unintelligibly; the photographer tears his hair.

But eventually, with coaxing from the photographer, the assistant, the PR and me, we get him out into the street. He flinches as the last rays of sunlight hit him and sinks into a doorway – luckily a very photogenic doorway – and the photographer clicks away. Every single person who passes down the street stops and says, 'Shane, good on yer!' or 'How're you doing?' A few bravely rush up and hug him. I didn't realise till then that he is a sort of god in Dublin – or not a god, more a prodigal son. Everyone seems to know him, everyone seems to love him, even little old ladies who surely can't ever have been Pogues fans shake their heads fondly and say, 'Shane! God love you!'

After the photographs, we stagger back to the hotel. I remark that the bar is terribly noisy – couldn't we sit somewhere else? Shane says, with sudden furious clarity, 'It's a bar. It's meant to be noisy.' The bar it is then – our home for the next six hours. Of all the Irish bars in all the world, this must be the most thoroughly charmless. It looks like a motorway Travelodge.

But it is Shane's bar and no doubt after his death it will be called 'Shane's Bar' – maybe the hotel will be rechristened 'Shane's Hotel'. Gin and tonics begin to appear as if by magic – rows and rows of them filling the table, perhaps materialised by fairy folk because I never see them coming.

I start by saying I very much enjoyed his book *A Drink with Shane MacGowan* – it is one of the freshest, most original biographies I've ever read. It's written as a conversation with his girlfriend, Victoria Mary Clarke, and it's a picture of their relationship as much as of his life. Shane, truculently, mumbles that it's not his book, and he is not happy with it. He doesn't like the title – 'A Drink with Shane MacGowan' is not accurate because of course it is many drinks over many years. And then he doesn't like the byline – why is he credited as co-author when it was all Victoria's work? It was just an interview, he insists, just her sometimes switching on the tape recorder when they were talking. And he doesn't 'stand by' anything he is quoted as saying because he might say one thing one day and something else the next.

So is he cross with her for writing the book? 'I can't be cross with her,' he says indignantly, 'I love her!' But he is cross with the book. And with the publishers, Sidgwick & Jackson. There is some ongoing saga whereby he claims they agreed to pay his hotel bill and haven't done so. They say they did agree to pay – for two days while he was doing interviews – not the six weeks (and counting) he has stayed there.

Anyway, he says ominously that he has not finished cutting the book. The press release claims that it recounts his days as a rent boy in London, but there is nothing about being a rent boy in the book. 'I can't believe you were a rent boy,' I say rudely, 'who would pay to rent you?' 'You'd be surprised,' he says. 'There are women who would climb over their grandmothers to get to a celebrity – Victoria, for instance!' and he emits the first of his exploding-coffee-machine laughs.

Where is Victoria now? 'Off ligging with U2 in London,' he says. She is Irish but prefers living in London – he prefers Dublin or Tipperary. He was meant to go to the U2 concert but couldn't face travelling to England. Travel must be a serious problem for him – Victoria in the book mentions the hours or even days spent in airports waiting to find a flight willing to take him. Once when he was booked to join Bob Dylan in the States, four flights came and went without him.

And yet Victoria is obviously devoted – she calls him 'Sweet Pea' throughout the book. They have been together fifteen years, so why haven't they married? 'Because we never had enough celebrities in the same place at the same time.' (This gnomic utterance is later explained by Victoria – they plan to sell their wedding to *Hello!* or *OK!* magazine.) 'But we're getting married this year. Hopefully.' And will they start a family? 'I think when we grow up we should [he is forty-three, she thirty-five] – it's something we've discussed. But probably I'm dropping myself in the shit even talking about it.'

His mother told him never to have children till he was rich. He was rich, he made millions with the Pogues, but he says now he's spent it all. 'If you hug money, you clog up the cash flow, know what I mean?' He says he's not destitute – he still gets enough from song-writing royalties to keep him in booze and fags – but he missed out on the rock-star mansions. All he owns is a flat in Gospel Oak which he shares with Victoria, and the old family farm in Tipperary which has no running water. His current group, the Popes, has never achieved success by Pogues standards. Supposing he never makes another record, will he have enough to live on? 'Well,' he sputters, 'I could always open supermarkets!'

The wit is quick and comes like a wake-up call to me, reminding me of Bono's remark, 'Shane is more together than people imagine.' (Bono obviously respects him, because he lent him his Martello Tower to live in for a year after the Pogues split up.) Shane's speech may be slurred, his movements uncoordinated, he sometimes gets stuck on saying, 'Know what I mean? Know what I mean? Know what I mean?' till you want to scream – but he is not 'out of it'. On the contrary, he seems to be controlling this interview much better than me. When he doesn't want to answer a question, he ignores it, or mumbles into his G & T. But every time he mentions an Irish name, he spells it out carefully, complete with accents, into my tape recorder. Moreover, unlike me, he remembers everything he says. This was brought sharply home a couple of hours into our conversation when the barman called him over to take a phone call. It was from Victoria and he came back saying, 'You've got to take out that line about her climbing over her grandmother to get to a celebrity. She didn't think it was funny. So take it out, or I'll fucking sue you, right?' (Later, in London, I persuaded Victoria to let me keep it in – she says it's OK because her grandmother is dead – but fancy him remembering.)

Shane sees it as his duty to educate me in Irish history, so I'm in for a lot of lecturing about Brian Ború, the Black and Tans, Michael Collins, Partition, 'Ireland is a woman', the craic, the whole tear-stained Emerald Isle package. And yet if you step outside Bloom's Hotel, you can see that Dublin today is just about the glossiest, yuppiest place in Europe – it has such full employment it actually has to import workers. Hasn't Shane noticed?

Evidently not. 'I live in the past. It doesn't feel like 2001 to me.' In any case, his Ireland is an entirely personal construct of songs and myths and stories his relatives told him in infancy, i.e. an Ireland that was probably extinct by the time he was born, if it ever even existed. He has lived in England since he was six – he won a scholarship to Westminster, for heaven's sake! (Admittedly only for a year, but still . . .) There are people who knew him in his teens who say he didn't have an Irish accent then. But, on the other hand, all his song-writing inspiration comes from Ireland and he achieved his 'crusade' with the Pogues to make Irish music hip and popular, to build Irish self-esteem. In fact, he was one of the founders of the current Irish cultural renaissance – it is just unfortunate that he looks more like a relic of the old pre-boom Ireland of hopeless old pissheads doing zilch.

Shane's father 'likes a drink', his uncles, aunts, cousins ditto. Shane claims that, when he was a small child in Tipperary, they gave him two Guinnesses a night as his bedtime drink and later, when he was eight, an uncle intro- duced him to Powers Whiskey. He says he never really drew a sober breath after the age of fourteen. 'In our family it was like, if the kid likes a drink, let him have a drink – because all the kids who weren't allowed to have a drink turned into raging alcoholics.' Mmm, yes, Shane – and . . .? Even he notices some logical flaw in his argument because he starts sputtering, 'We'd never even heard of alcoholism. We'd have thought it was some kind of weird religion. Our household was an open house where no one was refused, there was a continuous ceilidh going on, people would come from miles around for a drink, twenty-four hours, there's always one or two people awake.'

This was his mother's family's house in Tipperary, where he lived till he was six, while his parents worked in England. He says in the book, 'My life was a happy dream when I was a little boy.' But when he came to live with his parents in London, the picture grows darker and there are glimpses in the book of a deeply dysfunctional family – father out boozing every night, mother lying in bed with arthritis or depression, pilled out of her head, Shane trying to look after his little sister Siobhan. In the book he talks about his mother having a nervous breakdown but now he retracts that and says, 'I was just projecting, you know. I was depressed.'

When he was seventeen, he had a major breakdown and was admitted to a psychiatric hospital for six months. 'I was drinking a lot and I'd been put on a heavy prescription of tranquillisers by the GP. This was a big thing in the '70s – there's thousands of people in mental hospitals who were made zombies by downers. Anyway, they got me off the gear, the drugs that had put me there, and I started drinking again – but then they wouldn't let me drink, which is where the trouble started. It was called Acute Situational Anxiety – which basically meant I didn't like being in London. Perpetual panic – I panic in London.'

Does he panic about performing? 'No, that isn't the panic at all. My family were, are, all singers, performers. No, just sitting in a goddamn bloody flat in bloody London, that's a panic situation. Basically, I've been holding my breath half my fucking life. I can only relax when I'm in Ireland or one or two other places – Thailand, Spain, Japan and certain parts of America. I actually feel physically sick when I think of London.'

And yet, Victoria told me later he seemed happy enough living in London till Christmas, but then he went to Dublin for a Popes concert and never came back. He now claims to live in Tipperary, in the old family farmhouse with the sign on the door saying 'Trespassers will be shot'. His parents live in a new house down the road. He describes them as 'very young at heart, intelligent, warm, loving sociopaths'. (Everyone else describes them as 'characters'.) But actually he seems to have been living in Bloom's Hotel, Dublin, since January.

What it seems to boil down to is that he feels happy and sociable and safe drinking in Ireland, and depressed and lonely and paranoid drinking in London. But what about not drinking – is that ever a possibility? Yes, he says, 'I don't have to drink.' Victoria took him to the Priory last autumn for a dry-out and he says it worked. But, er, what are all these glasses on the table? 'This isn't drinking. We're just having a couple of drinks, you know?' Right. How long did he stay sober after the Priory? 'As long as it took to get to the nearest bar.' So is that his pattern – to dry out, then start drinking again? 'I don't have a pattern. I can't remember from one day to the next.'

At one point I said something about his attraction to drink and drugs, and he was suddenly beadily alert. 'What! I'm a drinker. I drink. But drugs, you said – I don't take drugs.' What? Never? 'So long ago I can't remember.' He should read Victoria's book, then, because it's full of drugs – uppers and downers and acid and cocaine. He once said that by the time the Pogues ended in 1991 he was taking 50 tabs of acid a day – 'You get used to it, you can function on it.'

But it has obviously become a touchy subject since November 1999, when Sinéad O'Connor shopped him to the police for taking heroin. She told the *Sun* she went round to his flat and found him practically in a coma on the floor and called the police because 'I love Shane and it makes me angry to see him destroy himself.' He says he was sitting peacefully on the sofa watching a Sam Peckinpah video. Whatever – no police charges were brought. So was he ever on heroin? 'What – addicted to heroin?' Well, on heroin? 'I've tried it a long time ago.' The only drugs he will admit to taking now are prescription tranquillisers – 'If the doctor prescribes them, I take them, and sometimes quite a heavy dose, for stress. But at least I go to a doctor, know what I mean?'

Midway through the evening, a man comes into the bar, sees Shane, and rushes over. Shane lurches to his feet and hugs him for a good five minutes. He is Gerry O'Boyle, former owner of Filthy MacNasty's bar in Islington, and they 'go back a long way'. Gerry rustles up a few more G & Ts but, I notice, drinks water. He stays with us for the rest of the evening, and Shane seems happy to have him. Later, when I am drunk as a skunk, Gerry serves the useful purpose of changing the tape when necessary.

At some point they decide to teach me how to say a rosary and both whip out their rosaries and an amazing array of medals and scapulas and plastic folders saying 'I am a Catholic. If I am dying, please call a priest.' Shane says he would certainly want a priest if he were dying. One reason why he likes St John of God – a Dublin drying-out home he some-times uses – is that it's run by nuns, and priests come round to hear your confession. 'I haven't been to mass for a long time.

But I pray every day, every night. I pray all the time. I pray whenever I'm struck by fear and worry, and I pray in gratitude when the release is given to me, you know?'

As a Catholic, doesn't he feel bad about not having children? 'I've got children!' How many? 'I don't know. I only know about one. He's a young man. He lives in Scotland. He knows where to get hold of me. I saw him once, when he was three. He knows I'm his father. Years ago, me and Lesley agreed that any time he wanted to come and see me he could come and see me and I'd take him out for a drink, get him whatever he wants. But she married a good man, and he seems to be satisfied with him as his father.'

Later in the evening Shane and Gerry announce that they have decided they can trust me, so they will cut me in on the bank robbery they are doing tomorrow. They are driving to a country town, about an hour out of Dublin, and they need a getaway driver. 'She'd be a fucking brilliant driver!' Shane opines. 'She'd be a good driver, yes,' Gerry agrees. 'Well, I don't know. I stop at zebra crossings. I'm rather a slow driver,' I warn them. Both nod eagerly. 'See, if you were a fast driver, it would be very obvious. A slow getaway driver is good!'

The evening reels on. Shane sings, 'Woman come in the name of love,' and ends with the plea, 'Can I not convince you to come out with us and rob a bank?' I tell him my husband wouldn't like it and he accepts that – obeying your husband is good. But, he suggests with great delicacy, perhaps my husband will die before me and then I can come out and rob a bank? I promise to think about it.

Gerry reminds Shane periodically that there's a party at the Clarence they should go to. 'You come!' Shane orders. 'I haven't got anything to wear,' I whimper – rather a feeble excuse in view of Shane's suit. 'Come as you are,' he says magnanimously. So several hours or aeons later, we stagger into the glossy streets of Temple Bar round to the Clarence, which luckily is only a few yards. Apparently *le tout* Dublin is there – Candace Bushnell and Marianne Faithfull and two Corrs! But my vision isn't too great by this stage and in a sudden flash of clarity I realise I must go to bed or I will die. I totter over to Shane and say, 'Gorra go,' and somehow the big friend from his hotel room appears at my elbow and steers me gently back to the hotel.

In the morning, badly hungover, I wander downstairs about nine to ask the receptionist what time I can decently phone Shane to say goodbye. 'Ask him,' she says cheerily. 'He's in the bar.' Omigod, he is – sitting at the bar with four or five G & Ts in front of him, chatting to the barman. The barman looks near death but Shane looks much as usual. 'Where were you?' he says quite sharply. 'You missed a good night.' Apparently he and his friends went from the party to a club to another party and another club, where he sang a few songs. Then they came back to talk. But now everyone else has gone to bed, and he is quite eager to start chatting all over again. But sorry, Shane, I just can't face it and anyway I have to catch a plane. I tell him it was a joy to meet him and he lurches to his feet and says with great formality, 'The pleasure's all mine.' What a well-brought-up boy!

Back in London, I immediately ring Victoria Clarke, agog to see what Shane's girlfriend can be like. She says she would love to meet but she's going to some place in Kennington for a five-day residential fast. Next day, however, she rings to say she is having a sauna at her health club in Hampstead and I can join her there. I drive there thinking – sauna, health club, fast – and this is Shane's girlfriend? My jaw actually drops when I meet her – she is peachy-skinned and milkmaid-wholesome, as fresh and glowing as a yogurt ad. How can she bear to marry an alky who by his own admission never takes a bath?

But she doesn't see Shane like that: she thinks he is beautiful. She first met him twenty years ago when she was fifteen and 'I thought he was gorgeous. At first I didn't like him as a person – I always fancied him, but thought he was really arrogant. I know he's not conventionally handsome but he is beautiful.' And yes, she confirms, they are getting married as soon as they can get someone to pay. 'I hear *Hello!* pay up to 500 grand! You've got to get lots of celebrities to come, though, for that.'

Gosh, what can I say? I just sit there gawping at her. But hasn't she noticed this, er, problem with Shane? Yes, she says calmly, she knows about alcoholism. She's been to AA and Al-Anon (she prefers AA, found Al-Anon 'very gloomy'). She thinks Shane could stop drinking if he wanted to – in fact, she says he drinks much less at home than when he's on show – part of his problem is social anxiety, which he covers up with booze. 'But I would hate it if someone said to me, "You've got to stop drinking." I love wine.'

In any case, she sympathises with addiction because she suffers it herself – she has a mild addiction to food and a major addiction to fame, and has had therapy for both. But now she plans to cure her fame addiction by hiring herself a publicist – she thinks probably Matthew Freud – to make her famous so she can get it out of her system. 'Because it's one of those things, like with heroin – you've got to try it before you can decide that you're going to give it up.'

But doesn't this fame obsession make her relationship with Shane a bit suspect? Doesn't he worry that she might leave him for someone more famous? 'I've already done that. [Apparently she had an affair with Van Morrison.] We've been through it, we've had the affairs, we've had the break-ups, we've had the nervous breakdowns. But with me it didn't last – the connection was never strong enough with anyone else – so it must be that I actually genuinely like him more than anyone else. And also we did meet before he was famous.'

Shane told me sweetly, 'I would never pretend to understand Victoria – or if I did understand her, I probably wouldn't love her, you know?' I do know. He is so lucky to have the love of a good woman, but at least he knows it – he writes in the foreword to her book, 'God bless the day I found her, and I feel like the luckiest fucker alive.' I hope they get married; I hope they live happily ever after. A few days later I bumped into Sir Bob Geldof at a party and asked him whether he thought *Hello!* would pay for their wedding. 'Well,' he said, 'I'll pay for it if *Hello!* won't – I just want to see it happen!' Me too – perhaps we should start a Victoria and Shane Wedding Appeal.

*

I felt, when I left Shane that morning in Dublin, that he could not live much longer – in fact he's still flourishing and finally married to the wonderful Victoria. But my meeting with him is weirdly connected in my memory with my husband's death in 2003. David was only fifty-nine; he looked about forty; there was absolutely nothing visibly wrong with him. But he'd had a slight prostate condition which meant he had to have regular blood tests and in late 2002 one of these tests revealed that he had myelofibrosis, a degenerative disease of the bone marrow. The doctors said that he had 'only two good years' (they didn't specify how many bad ones) unless he had a bone marrow transplant, and the sooner the better. There was then a very nail-biting period when they were testing his brothers to see which one should be the donor, in the course of which David casually revealed that he didn't believe they were his brothers anyway – he thought his mother had had a wartime fling. But luckily they were, and David went into UCH to have the transplant in July. He was still perfectly fit – we'd been to a wedding in Northern Ireland the weekend before and danced the night away. And a month later he was dead. His kidneys failed in the course of the chemo so he was on dialysis and then he suffered a bleed to the brain that killed him overnight. He was meant to be coming home the next week.

It was such a shock I was effectively insane for several months. At first I was passive, glued to my armchair, obsessively going over the details of David's last few weeks in hospital. That was relatively standard widow behaviour, I think. But after a while this was replaced by a really florid madness, a peculiar I-can-do-anything triumphalism that seemed to be based on the idea: I'll show him I can manage without him! I made long to-do lists and – this was the unusual bit – actually did them. I had the house redecorated and rehung pictures, I sold old furniture and bought new, I replanned the front garden and built a fence, I learned to cook. I was a hideous mad tornado of energy, rather like Mrs Thatcher – off with the old, on with the new, can't hang about, why put off till tomorrow what you can do today, etc etc. I even contemplated moving house – thank God I didn't – because everyone told me that's what widows were meant to do. 'You don't want to sit there, being reminded of David at every turn.' Actually that's precisely what I did want to do, and the idea that you could forget someone you were married to for over thirty years, or would want to, simply by moving house is completely absurd. But anyway I obediently went round estate agents and looked at flats in Docklands (in Docklands!) and thought I could embark on a whole new life. It was only when an estate agent exhorted me to stand on a chair and lean right out of the window so that I could see the 'river view' that some vestige of sanity returned, and I went home to my cats Samson and Delilah and assured them, 'Don't worry, we're not moving anywhere.'

The *Observer* meanwhile, trying to be helpful, kept suggesting bereaved people for me to interview, thinking it would be a gentle way back to work. I eventually agreed to interview Jane Clark, widow of Alan Clark, at Saltwood Castle. The idea, I think, was that we would bond over the loss of our husbands and perhaps shed a few companionable tears. In fact – but I must stress that I was still completely bonkers at this stage – she filled me with alarm. She said that whenever she was feeling depressed or lost, she sat on Alan's grave (a large boulder in the garden) and talked to him. Yikes! It was *four years* since Alan Clark's death, and I thought: God, I hope I'm not still maundering on about David in four years' time. One year, I thought, would be quite enough time to spend mourning. (I was wrong about that.) But anyway I went back to the office screeching, 'She's a nutter!' till the editor tactfully advised me to tone it down. But I think he realised, as I did, that the idea that I could 'use' my bereavement to develop a new line in touchy-feely interviews was a non-starter. I have never done touchy-feely interviews and have never felt the need to, mainly because I think there are so many other journalists who can do them better. And also I hate to see people crying (I very rarely cry myself) and am apt to say things like 'Brace up!' which never go down well.

But meanwhile, all through this energy-insanity period, I lay awake at night haunted by the promise I'd made to Shane MacGowan that, if I were ever widowed, I would help him rob a bank. I had made the promise in perfectly good faith (safe, I thought, in the certainty that my husband would outlive me) and I didn't like to break my word. Shane was bound to know I'd been widowed and would be wondering why I hadn't yet come to Dublin. Should I book a flight tomorrow? Should I ring him first or just turn up? Would I be any good as a bank robber's getaway driver, or would I stall at the first traffic lights? What did I feel about robbing a bank – I didn't mind robbing a bank per se but presumably the money was meant to go to the IRA and did I actually want to support the IRA? Would I mind being caught – I felt we were bound to be – and going to prison? And if I did go to prison, what would happen to my cats? Ah – salvation. My cats seem to have acted as my lifeline to sanity throughout this period. I couldn't rob a bank with Shane MacGowan because then I would go to prison and my cats would be put down. Problem solved. Nevertheless I played the Pogues obsessively for months and felt a lingering guilt that I broke my promise to rob a bank with Shane MacGowan.

CHAPTER NINE

Sex with Michael Winner

I used to interview Michael Winner at any opportunity, partly because he was such good fun but also because I was intrigued by him. I felt I was within a hair's breadth of understanding his character but never quite got there. He readily agreed that his monster mother, 'Mumsy', was the root of all his problems but on the other hand he didn't think he *had* any problems. And in a way he didn't. He was fun to be with, he had plenty of friends, he believed he had achieved the perfect lifestyle. But he did once admit to me that he regretted not having children – 'That is the one mistake that wipes out everything I have ever done.'

He also had an extremely twisted attitude to money which I think accounts for why he never had children. Winner's father made a lot of money from property and was a serious art collector – he paid the world-record price for a Jan von Os flower painting and had a museum-quality collection of jade. He left it all to his widow, but Winner assumed that, as the only child, he would eventually inherit. Unfortunately he reckoned without Mumsy's gambling habit. She virtually lived in the casino at Cannes. And when she died in 1984, the thirty-five crates that were meant to contain his father's jade collection were found to contain only light bulbs and toilet paper – she had gambled everything away.

By that stage, Winner had made plenty of money himself, from films and property, but he still felt bitter about the lost inheritance. It was a reminder that women, even women who claimed to love you, could steal everything away. If you married, you might end up having to pay alimony. I think it's significant that he only finally got married at seventy-five, when his fortune had been eroded by the property crash and he was facing serious debts. And, after his death, it emerged that many of his staff and ex-girlfriends who thought they'd been provided for in his will had been left nothing at all. Even his widow, Geraldine, had to worry about paying the electricity bill.

Most of my interviews with Winner were ostensibly about food and conducted over lunch, which was always a great performance. I remember a scene at the Wolseley when he actually made Jeremy King (the co-owner) get out a tape measure and measure our table because he believed it was smaller than the one next to it. It wasn't; it was the same size. There was another hilarious scene at Assegai, a restaurant near his home in Holland Park which he never reviewed because he didn't want the hoi polloi coming. I asked him why he liked the restaurant particularly and he said, 'Oh because it attracts a very good class of person.' So saying, he glanced round and saw what I'd been able to see for some time – a woman breast-feeding her baby at the next table. I thought he might have a heart attack there and then, he was so shocked.

The following interview is the last one I ever did with him and unusual because it took place at his home and did not involve food. Instead, *Observer Woman* magazine asked me to find out about his sex life and his attitude to women. This seemed a slightly dodgy subject, given that he was seventy-two and in poor health but, as always, he was happy to oblige.

From the *Observer*, 4 November 2007

Michael Winner certainly should know about women because he has been tended by them for seventy-two years. The current cast is Geraldine Lynton-Edwards who has recently been promoted to fiancée, Dinah May his assistant, various cooks, maids, secretaries and cleaners, followed by an army of ex-girlfriends wending back into the mists of time. He claims to adore women – 'There's no question, women are nicer, kinder people.' On the other hand, he has never actually gone so far as to marry one. 'I have some congenital defect that prevents me marrying,' he explains. But that just possibly might be about to change . . .

So I trot round to his vast Kensington mansion to see how wedding plans are progressing, if at all. The maid opens the door and summons Dinah, who shows me to the private cinema downstairs. It has two old director's chairs saying 'Michael Winner', and walls and walls of photographs of Winner with the stars he is so boringly besotted by – Marlon Brando, Orson Welles, Burt Lancaster, Robert Mitchum, John Gielgud, Diana Rigg, Sophia Loren, Charles Bronson. Presumably he has chosen to meet me in the screening room because he likes to remind people that he was a film director – something I always find it politer to forget. His tape recorder is already laid beside his chair (he always tapes his interviews) and Dinah brings coffee for me and peach juice for him.

I was expecting him to look frail because he'd told me on the phone, 'I'm crippled for life, darling,' but even so I am shocked when he limps into the room. His hands shake; his voice is wheezy; he seems altogether shrunken. This is all as a result of the terrible (and terribly obscure) illness Vibrio vulnificus that he contracted in Barbados at New Year. He was flown back in an air ambulance and not expected to live. He was in the London Clinic for five and a half months, and had nineteen operations, one of which removed .his Achilles tendon leaving him with a permanent limp. There is a terrible irony in the fact that he has just published a book, *The Fat Pig Diet*, which proudly recounts how he lost three and a half stone last year by following his self-invented diet – eat less, eat early – but everyone will assume he lost the weight through illness.

But just when I'm thinking: Poor thing – I mustn't tire him, he starts shouting at about 1,000 decibels, 'Di-nah! Di-nah!' and she comes running back. It turns out he wants a radiator switched off which I could have done if he'd explained, but anyway she turns it off and he gives her time to get back upstairs before bellowing again, 'Di-nah! Di-nah! Oh God!' This time he explains, 'She hasn't pulled all the curtains back. I asked her to do it and she hasn't done it. I'm a real old finicky arsehole, darling.' I can do it, I tell him. 'No. I like people to do what they're fucking well told. Di-nah!' So poor Dinah comes running back and he makes her draw all the curtains. (These aren't even window curtains, just sound-proofing curtains round the cinema screen.) 'Difficult patient, is he?' I ask Dinah and she rolls her eyes while Winner bellows, 'Difficult, darling! Difficult patient! Hahaha. Don't say a word, Dinah! The truth must not come out! Oh, she's wonderful, Dinah.'

Finally poor Dinah is allowed to go. She has worked for him for over twenty years so she must be used to it by now. I asked if she was an ex-girlfriend but he said no, she was already married when she came to him but, 'If I'd known her before she was married, I'm sure she would have been an ex-girlfriend!' Ex-girlfriend, I should explain, has a particular significance in Winnerworld. It is the equivalent to being, say, the fifth wife of a polygamous king who is now on to wife thirty-seven – it means you have been superseded but not forgotten and still retain a certain status. Winner boasts that he remains friends with all his ex-girlfriends though his *Fat Pig Diet* book slightly gives the lie to this when he recounts how a woman recently came up to him in St Alban restaurant in Regent Street and said hello and he asked her name and she said, 'You should know. I slept with you for a year!' But that, he explains, was unusual – 'I'd lost track of her. I haven't kept in touch with all of them, darling. But I'm on the phone to about two or three every day. Every day. Certain ones more than others. It's a great pleasure. People say I've never had a family but I do have a family – a family of choice who I still adore, and help. Some of them have fallen on bad times or had illnesses – two are very ill actually and I pay all their bills.'

How many ex-girlfriends does he have altogether? 'Well we did a count and funnily enough, it was very low, about a hundred and thirty. That's not a lot! How can it be a lot for fifty years? Any self-respecting rock star gets through that in a day. Hahahaha. And they're bloody nice people.' But if they were so nice, why did he keep changing them? 'Because I was a pig in my behaviour – as well as becoming a fat pig later – in that I could never resist temptation. So if I was with somebody and somebody else became available, I would have them. When I look back on the way I behaved, I feel sickened, absolutely sickened. I think: That person was loyal, decent, loved me – how could I have done that? And not really had any conscience about it? I mean openly going off with other people? It was cruel. And it was purely motivated by greed. They were all bloody nice people – I mean there were a few one-night stands in Hollywood and all that sort of stuff – but on the whole anyone I spent any time with was a really decent, terrific person.'

When were the one-night stands? In the 1960s? 'Well all the time, dear. I would never reject a one-night stand. I wasn't looking for them so much later on, but occasionally they'd turn up.' Wasn't he worried about catching something? 'Well . . . obviously not. And I never did catch anything. Quite early on I found I had quite a low sperm count so the chances of having a child were almost nil.' Did he ever pay for sex? 'Never. Never ever ever. First of all, I'm too mean and it wasn't necessary because I was getting it free. And the girls I've had were much prettier! Why should I trade in an Aston Martin for a battered 1936 Ford and pay for it?'

His detractors might assume that Winner's women were all gold-diggers who chased him for his money but 'That is nonsense!' he insists – it was for his lovely bubbly personality. 'Girls want to be entertained. They want to have a fun day. It's no fun being with a very rich man if he's unbelievably boring.' And anyway he was chased by rich women as well.

One was the author of *The Beverly Hills Diet*, who pursued him with pineapples back in the 1970s: 'I would arrive at an airport somewhere and a chauffeur would appear with this enormous bag of pineapples. She thought pineapples were the way to my heart! Did she have the wrong number! I hate pineapples!'

But why was he always so reluctant to commit? Most of his girlfriends believe it was the baleful influence of Mumsy, Helen Winner, a compulsive gambler who spent all his inheritance in the Cannes casino and then took to suing him for more cash – it was one of her lawsuits, he believes, that brought on his first heart attack. He saw women as a threat to his money and he does care a lot about money: it is vital to his *amour-propre* to be a very rich man. 'It's a dreadfully mean thing to say, but I used to see flashing above girlfriends' heads "Alimony. Alimony. Alimony". I would think to myself realistically three out of four marriages fail and my chances won't be any better than anybody else's and probably worse. So do I really want to give away millions of pounds? Which is a terrible thing to say. But I just never wanted to get married. And they were wonderful people. The only one who behaved as appallingly as I did was Jenny Seagrove.'

And yet the actress Jenny Seagrove was the one he came closest to marrying. He auditioned her for a part in his movie *Appointment with Death* in 1987 and rang her agent and said, 'I have two offers. Firstly, I wish to marry Jenny Seagrove. Secondly, I want her in the movie.' She got the part in the movie, but she couldn't marry Winner because she was already married to an Indian actor called Madhav Sharma who refused a divorce. (This could explain Winner's willingness to propose.) And when she eventually got a divorce, Winner somehow failed to marry her though they lived together for six and a half years. She left him in 1993 just two weeks before he was going into hospital for a triple heart bypass. So she behaved pretty badly? 'Oy vey! I couldn't walk 30 yards without breathing problems and she left. She wasn't nice then. But I had not been nice before so you have to make allowances. She went off with Bill Kenwright [the theatrical impresario], and I remember saying to a very famous actress, "I'm sure that all happened afterwards," and she said, "No, no, I can tell you, Michael – there were rehearsals going on." Hahaha. But it doesn't matter because I did it first.'

They are only just on speaking terms again. 'A few years ago, a mutual friend said Jenny would love to have a chat. So I wrote her a card and said love to see you sometime to have a chat. To which I got an answer eight weeks later: "I don't feel quite ready for a chat yet." That was after we'd been apart for three years! I wasn't asking for a blowjob! And then the same thing happened the other day – a mutual friend said she's so keen to talk to you, she wants to know your mobile. I said I don't have a mobile and she knows the phone number – she lived here for six and a half years. So then she says to this fellow, "Well I don't think this is the time to call him. And if I do call him, he'll ask me out to dinner." So I said Emil, can you take a letter: "Dear Jenny, May I make it clear that I do not wish to have dinner with you, nor do I wish to have breakfast, lunch, tea, or night-time cocoa. But I wish you well." And then – humiliated by this letter which I sent through an intermediary, hahahaha

– she rang me at five to one, when she knows I always have lunch at one, and we had a very nice chat. But that was the first time in eight years.'

Anyway, all this mad pursuit is now in the past because, at seventy-two, for the first time in his life he is engaged. The lucky girl is Geraldine Lynton-Edwards who has been his girl-friend for several years but is now officially his fiancée. Perhaps 'girl' is a bit of a misnomer – Winner admits that he met her in 1957 when he was making his first movie. 'I spent a day interviewing people in my father's office near Olympia and next day the secretary rings here and says, "There's a girl turned up for the interview." I said, "Well, that was yester-day." And – I'll never forget the way she said it – she said, "I think you'd like to see her." So I thought: Oooh! And I walked round to the office and there was Geraldine, and we had an affair then, and we've seen each other from time to time over the years.' Hang on, hang on! I cry. He met her fifty years ago? So how old is she? I've always assumed she was in her early fifties. 'Oh listen, she annoys me greatly. She looks like a well-preserved fifty and she keeps telling everyone she's sixty-eight or sixty-nine or whatever she is! I say, "Why are you telling them this? Keep your bloody mouth shut!" Because she looks incredible. At all times! And she hasn't had plastic surgery or anything.'

Anyway they had an affair half a century ago, then she moved to Paris, married, had children (she is now a grand-mother) but, like any good ex-girlfriend, kept in touch. When she moved back to London a few years ago, she started seeing Winner again and became the reigning girlfriend. She was the one who got him dieting and doing Pilates and walking for one hour a day. All his friends agreed that she was very good for him. But of course he could never resist temptation and in the spring of 2005 he had a fling with 'Princess' (not really) Paola Lombard and Geraldine went off to Milan to teach at her sister's dance school. The affair with Paola only lasted a few months and very shortly afterwards she was diagnosed with breast cancer. To the cynical eye it might look as if Winner left Paola Lombard because she had cancer but he insists, 'Ohnonono. She didn't have cancer when we fell out. Oh I would never leave anyone like that. We fell out and then two weeks later she discovered she had cancer. She still is unbelievably unwell and I support her completely. I haven't seen her for over a year – because I think it's a very delicate issue for Geraldine – but I speak to her on the phone.'

Paola having departed, he immediately invited Geraldine back but she said no, she had promised to stay in Milan for a year. But she returned in July 2006 and has been with him ever since. She has her own flat, but has been living with him since his illness and has been 'a beacon and saviour' throughout. 'She was unbelievable during this illness. I said I've been in hospital for five months and she said, "So have I." I mean she would get me food, help me get dressed, she did everything, she was incredible. You couldn't have asked anyone to do more – or expected as much. She is a remarkable person.' Would he do the same for her if she were ill? 'Well, I would wish to look after her, and I think I would, yes I would. Because I love her and I would have to. I wouldn't desert her. I wouldn't say, "Well this is getting rather boring now, I'll go somewhere else." '

'I thought maybe you would?'

142

'No! I don't think I would. No, that would be really horrible.'

So Geraldine's reward for her loyalty is to be made official fiancée. Are they busy making plans for their wedding? 'No! Listen – I said to her it's taken me seventy-two years to get engaged, so don't hold your breath for the wedding! She took it very well. It's enough we got engaged – I'm still in shock from that.' Even so, I have a hunch he might amaze his friends by getting married eventually. He seems to have given some thought to it. For instance, I asked whether, if they did marry, he would want it to be in a synagogue? 'No – you can't be less Jewish than Geraldine Lynton-Edwards, darling. She is, as they say, the shiksa of all time. And she ain't going to convert. That takes a long time and I wouldn't wish her to. No, we'd find some moron who's licensed to make people man and wife.' I reckon a nice juicy offer from *Hello!* or *OK!* for the wedding exclusive could swing it.

Is he still up for sex? 'Well, I'm up for sex to a somewhat lesser degree than I used to be, hahahaha! I'm certainly not looking for it. This is the first time in my life – since the return of Geraldine – the first time ever that I'm not looking to have an affair. I don't wish to have an affair, I don't wish to be unfaithful. And it's taken seventy-two years to reach this point of god-like tranquillity. As far as I'm concerned, that's it.'

*

He died on 21 January 2013. We knew he was dying because he had stopped writing his *Sunday Times* restaurant reviews a few weeks before, which meant he must be very near the end.

But at least he did not die a bachelor – he had married Geraldine in September 2011, with his dear friends Michael and Shakira Caine as witnesses. It took him seventy-five years to pluck up the courage to commit but at least he did it.

CHAPTER TEN

Writers

I was a very bookish child. I remember whole school holidays in which I did nothing but read – mainly because there was nothing else to do. I hoovered up Enid Blyton, Georgette Heyer, Conan Doyle, Agatha Christie and all the great crime novelists. I liked writers who wrote a *lot* – Simenon was a great find – because it meant I could trot down to the public library every Saturday and be sure of finding another four Christies or another four Heyers. On Saturdays I also went to Boots the Chemist to collect romantic novels (Barbara Cartland and suchlike) for my grandmother, who lived with us, but I never attempted to read them. My mother had more elevated tastes – she read mainly historical novels, and put me on to Margaret Irwin, Mary Renault, and *Gone with the Wind*. My father meanwhile was reading every book ever published (this is before he went blind) on Roman history, and the First and Second World Wars. The net result was that if you came to 52 Clifden Road, Twickenham almost any evening you would find four people with their noses in a book. Eventually, when my grandmother was bedridden, Dad rented a television for her and would sometimes go up to her room to watch it, but Mum and I rarely if ever did.

Reading was no hardship for me so it was obvious that I should study Eng Lit when I went to Oxford. By then, I had read most of the nineteenth-century novelists so I assumed it would just be more of the same. Anglo-Saxon (and, even worse, Middle English) came as a nasty shock. But the main trouble was that at Oxford I discovered there were so many more enjoyable things to do. Why spend an afternoon with Spenser's beastly *Faerie Queene* when I could spend it at a *fête champêtre* on the Cherwell? I read enough to get a second, but began to resent books as things that interfered with more exciting pleasures, and spent most of my twenties avoiding them. It was only when I had children that I rediscovered the luxury of reading – after chasing toddlers all day, an evening with a book became my idea of the highest self-indulgence. It was not until my thirties that I was able to catch up on all the books I'd missed at school and Oxford when I was locked into the English syllabus. This was when I discovered the Russian novelists, when I read Proust and *Madame Bovary* for the first time, and inched my way into the American canon by way of Henry James. At Oxford, we'd been given the impression that novel-writing stopped with Thomas Hardy, and never crossed the Atlantic, so it was a joy to find Scott Fitzgerald and all the great American novelists waiting for me.

The Great American Novel that probably made the most impact on my generation was *Catch-22*, so I was thrilled, in 1998, to be able to interview its author, Joseph Heller. He was by then very old, in poor health, and publishing a feeble auto-biography called *Now and Then* which should have warned me of disappointment to come. But when I rang him from New York, I was still trembling with excitement. He told me to take the jitney to Long Island and get off at Amagensett, where he would meet me at the bus stop. When I arrived, the rain was bucketing down, but there was no sign of Joseph Heller. I think I saw him drive past and come back fifteen minutes later when I was soaked to the skin. That would have been his idea of a good joke. He and his wife took me to a restaurant and proceeded to shout at each other over lunch, while I cowered between them and counted the minutes till I could catch the jitney back. It was a truly horrible experience and means that now, when I see *Catch-22* on my bookshelf, I shudder.

In theory, writers should be easy to interview because at least they speak intelligible English and use words accurately. On the other hand they tend to be quite secretive for the very good reason that they regard their own lives as material that they might want to use themselves. Why should they squander it on journalists who are bound to muck it up? But they also resent any suggestion that the characters or scenes in their novels could be based on their own lives.

I remember interviewing Muriel Spark in 1990 and feeling it was like inching up a rock face. She was perfectly friendly but she gave almost nothing away. On the other hand, I felt it was one of the most worthwhile interviews I ever did in that what little bits and pieces I discovered were genuinely 'new' and of value to future biographers. She wouldn't talk about her short-lived disastrous marriage to Ossie Spark, who went mad in Rhodesia – 'He's still alive, poor thing' – but she talked about why she never remarried: 'Sexually, probably, I could be faithful: that's not the point. The point is I couldn't concentrate on the job, I really couldn't. I'm too interested in my writing: I couldn't *work* at a marriage.'

Later, I got to know her a bit better when she asked me and my family to cat-sit her house in Tuscany. It was teeming with fleas so we all hated it, but we liked the area so much we rented a nearby (flea-free) house every summer and invited Muriel and her companion Penelope Jardine over for meals. Penelope, a sculptor, wore the sort of casual clothes we all wore in Tuscany, but Muriel always dressed more formally in one of her many silk dresses with a piece of 'good' jewellery. So I was alarmed one day when she suggested taking me to her favourite dress shop in Valdarno. Penelope, as always, drove; Muriel sat beside her and sang hymns most of the way – she had a sweet voice.

The dress shop was everything I feared, with over-attentive sales assistants forcing me to try ever more horrendous (and horrendously expensive) silk dresses with matching coats, the sort of 'mother of the bride' clothes I would not be seen dead in. But Muriel was nothing if not determined. She made me try practically everything in the shop and kept telling me I would get a good discount – I had to buy some trousers eventually just to escape. Perhaps she was trying to encourage me into the sort of self-transformation she accomplished in Rome in the late 1960s, after the success of *Jean Brodie*, when she went from being a dumpy, frumpy, middle-aged woman to a dazzlingly chic slim beauty who was coiffed to the nines and dressed in couture. It didn't work with me.

Muriel Spark had not yet written her autobiography, *Curriculum Vitae*, when I interviewed her – it might have helped if she had. With my next interviewee, Hilary Mantel, I at least had the advantage of knowing about her childhood from her brilliant memoir, *Giving Up the Ghost*. But we have only a patchy knowledge of her adult life. We know about her illness, endometriosis, because she has talked about it often in interviews. And we know a bit about her stay in Saudi Arabia because she wrote a novel, *Eight Months on Ghazzah Street*, set there. There is a big blank, though, about her life in Botswana and I wanted to find out about that. She of course wanted to talk about the Tudors.

Alas, I am probably the only person in the world who is not a fan of *Wolf Hall* and *Bring Up the Bodies*. I know they both won Man Booker Prizes, I know that zillions of readers (including men who normally never read novels) were gripped by them, but I much prefer her previous, non-historical fiction. This probably stems from my deep hatred of history – I decided at school that it was bunk and have never felt any need to change that view. You will tell me, of course – or you will if you are a public-school product of a certain age – that those who do not study history are doomed to repeat it, but I haven't noticed myself burning any witches lately.

The former *Times* editor, Sir Peter Stothard, when awarding the Man Booker Prize to Hilary Mantel, said that she had 'recast the most essential period of our modern history'. And, he added, 'I don't think there are many more important things a novelist can do.' The most essential period of our modern history? The Tudors? Seriously? Didn't we have a couple of world wars since then? And the idea that recasting history is the most important thing a novelist can do is equally bonkers – surely the greatest novelists try to write about the society they live in?

Anyway, I approached my interview with Hilary Mantel nervously, wondering how we could discuss *Wolf Hall* and

Bring Up the Bodies without my revealing my complete ignorance of the Tudors. I think she sussed. I think she susses *everything*. I think she is an exceptionally observant woman. But luckily also a kind one.

From the *Sunday Times*, 13 May 2012

Hilary Mantel has the most deceptive appearance of anyone I've ever met. She looks rather like a gerbil, soft and plump and fluffy, but it is safer to think of her as, say, a ferret or possibly even a tiger – something fierce that might bite you. Even her plumpness is misleading. It does not betoken a love of cake or chocolate but years of medication for endometriosis – until her twenties she was spikily thin. And although her speech sounds a bit quavering, I realised when I came to transcribe our interview that she speaks in perfect sentences, in perfect paragraphs, and entirely, sharply, to the point.

We met at her club, the Royal and Overseas in St James's, where she stays when she is in London. She apologised for not inviting me to her home in Devon but said she had a difficult week ahead, looking after a disabled cousin who had just sold her house and was about to move into a care home. 'And she's likely to be in poor shape – she'll have had a long journey, and given up her home. So I need to be on my own with her.' She admits, though, that it's bad timing with her book launch coming up.

Three years ago, when she won the Man Booker prize for *Wolf Hall*, Mantel said that she was working on a sequel, to be called *The Mirror and the Light*, which would follow Thomas Cromwell's career to his execution in 1540.

But it hasn't worked out that way. Her new novel, *Bring Up the Bodies*, finishes with the execution of Anne Boleyn, and there will then be a third volume taking us to Cromwell's death. 'When I got deeply into this one, I just realised that the drama had gathered such power, the reader is going to want to pause and not rush on to the next wife. And when I wrote those words "Bring up the bodies", it was like an electric shock – I thought this is a book and this is the title!'

Wolf Hall took her five years to write, but *Bodies* came much faster because she had already done most of the research and, she says, it's 'so short' – though still over 400 pages. 'I had this huge stack of handwritten material and I knew the book was in it somewhere but then I had to sit down and pull it together which I suppose took about six months.' She never starts with chapter one, but simply jots down scenes or bits of dialogue as they occur to her, in the notebooks she carries with her always, and then puts them in order at the end. 'So when my publishers ask, "Where are you up to?" I say, "All I can do is weigh it!" '

Many authors claim to be almost paralysed with fear after winning the Booker, but not Mantel: 'Actually it's been entirely positive for me. I just thought: Oh good, they're giving me a big cheque!' She had always found Septembers difficult, waiting for the announcement of the Booker shortlist, but she never even made the shortlist until *Wolf Hall*, though many critics expected her to for *Beyond Black* in 2005. 'And now I don't have to go through that again. It's something you want to achieve – and then the second phase of your career begins. And you feel freer.'

The £50,000 Booker cheque – and all the enhanced royalties when *Wolf Hall* became an international bestseller – enabled her and her husband Gerald McEwen to move to Budleigh Salterton in Devon. For twenty years they'd lived in an apartment in a huge converted lunatic asylum called Florence Court near Woking. But she wanted to be by the sea, and 'It was a time of change in our lives anyway. My husband had been very ill with peritonitis and it was a fullscale surgical emergency – life was turned upside down in an hour. And when he came out of hospital he didn't really want to go back to work. He'd been working twenty years as an IT consultant and I think he felt that's enough. So then *Wolf Hall* and the Booker enabled me to say well OK don't go back to work, come and work for me. He took over the business side of things, and he's the road manager, and he really looks after me.' Apparently he drives her everywhere in silence, while she sits in the back of the car, writing. She writes everywhere, even on holiday; she never stops.

The move to Devon brought other changes too. At Florence Court she was just Mrs McEwen – none of their neighbours knew she was a writer. 'I'd hardly ever admit to being a writer, because of the reactions you get from people. They say things like "Do you pay them to publish you?" Or "Do you do children's books?" Or they say, "I've always thought if I had the time I'd like to write a book." So I found it better to pretend to be a lady of leisure. And we lived surrounded by retired people who filled their days with golf so they were completely incurious – and that was fine by me. But life's different now we've moved to Devon. I'm involved with the literary festival and there's quite an active cultural life. So now people know what I do.'

The best guide to who she is and what she does is her wonderful memoir, *Giving Up the Ghost*, which she published in 2003. She started writing it because her stepfather died, and she was packing up his things and making notes about each object and eventually found that the notes were 'really about Jack's death, and I found it easing me back. So it hardly seems that I made a conscious decision that it was time to write a memoir. Of course it was mainly about childhood, it wasn't in any way a complete account of my life – which wouldn't have been interesting. And in a way it was private writing, explaining things to myself. You know they say never apologise, never explain and I think if you're a really strong person, that's the philosophy that could guide your life. But I'm not like that, and I wanted to explain.'

In particular, she wanted to explain the disappearance of her father, Henry. She was born in 1952 in Derbyshire, and lived in the village of Hadfield, near Glossop, surrounded by relatives – she was part of a vast Irish Catholic family. When Hilary was six or seven, her mother took in a lodger, Jack Mantel, and her father – who was always very retiring anyway – somehow retired into the spare room. And then when they moved house, to Cheshire, when she was eleven, they simply left her father behind – she never saw him again. Only when she published her memoir did she learn what happened to him. Apparently he married a widow with six children and the eldest daughter wrote to tell her that he died in 1997, but that he had seen her on television once and was proud of her.

Mantel once said that the loss of contact with her father came 'surprisingly low down' on her list of regrets, but she told me that was not quite correct: 'I think what I meant was that by the time the parting of the ways came, I had come to despise my father, and it was only later that I very much regretted that we had lost touch. Perhaps it's only when you're an adult it comes home to you, what's lost. I didn't ever feel that I was Jack Mantel's daughter, whereas my brothers thought of themselves as his sons. So I feel unfathered.'

Her brothers are five and six years younger, so I wondered if they could actually have been Jack Mantel's sons, but she says firmly, 'They could have been – but they weren't.' But they have no memories of their father because they were so young when he disappeared. She is very close to them, and sometimes emails them several times a day, but 'I often feel that we are half a generation apart rather than five or six years. Because they grew up very remote from the kind of childhood I had. I lived in Hadfield till I was eleven, and thought of myself as part of a huge Irish family because my grandmother's many many brothers and sisters were still alive. But by the time I was ten, most of them had died and my younger brothers don't remember those people, and don't have any consciousness of being Irish. Their lives started in a much more middle-class community with different expectations.'

The move to Cheshire was only eight miles but it meant a complete break from Hadfield, because Jack and her mother needed to make a fresh start. They told Hilary to change her surname to Mantel and to say Jack was her father. And she started at a new school, where she ended up as head girl and became the first member of her family to go to university. Her mother had had to leave school at fourteen and work in the mill like everyone else, but she was ambitious for Hilary: 'She encouraged me to think I was intelligent and that I would have chances, if she could provide them.'

Hilary went to the LSE to read law, but after a year of feeling lonely in London she decided to switch to Sheffield University to join McEwen, her boyfriend, who was reading geology there. They married when they were just twenty. But by then she was suffering from a whole clutch of symptoms – headaches, nausea, asthma, pains in her legs and abdomen – that her doctor saw as psychosomatic. He sent her to a psychiatrist, who prescribed stronger and stronger pills – Valium, Fentazin, Largactil, Stelazine – until eventually she had a fullscale nervous breakdown. In consequence, she resolved never to go near a psychiatrist or psychotropic drug again. She had hoped to become a barrister and eventually a politician – she was 'seethingly ambitious' – but she realised she would never have the stamina for such a career, so she thought: Well, better get a book up your sleeve because even if you're sick you can write.

She and her husband moved to Botswana for his work and she wrote her first novel there – a 900-page tome called *A Place of Greater Safety*, set in the French Revolution. But it was rejected by all the publishers she sent it to and only published eventually in 1992. She thinks if *Place* had been published at the time she would have stuck to writing historical fiction, but she says in those days historical fiction was seen as 'chick lit in long frocks' whereas *Place* was essentially political. So then she 'changed her strategy' and wrote a string of contemporary novels, starting with *Every Day Is Mother's Day* in 1985, which established her as a rising literary star.

While writing her novel in Botswana, she also read up medical textbooks and eventually diagnosed herself with endometriosis – a disease of the uterus but with ramifications all over the body. So when she came back to England for Christmas in 1979, she took herself to St George's Hospital who confirmed the diagnosis, but said the disease was so advanced the only treatment was removal of her ovaries and uterus. So, at twenty-seven, she lost any chance of motherhood. At the time, she didn't particularly want children but now she says, 'I miss the child I never had,' and wishes she'd had a baby at eighteen, when she thinks she still could have done: 'It wouldn't necessarily have stopped the endometriosis, but at least I would have had a child.'

Mysteriously, she divorced her husband while they were in Botswana and then remarried him two years later, but she won't explain why. 'I can't really talk about it. I might go back and write about it some time but in a disguised way. I do not think that things would have happened in the way they did if we'd been at home in England. We were very vulnerable, because we were far from family and friends. If you wanted to phone Britain – if the phones were working at all – you rang South Africa and asked them to place a call for you. Letters might or might not get there. You felt as though you might as well have been on another planet. And ours was not by any means the only marriage that disintegrated – it was almost normal. The most amazing thing was the way people ran off with the most unlikely partners, never to be heard of again. That whole society, that expat way of life and how it affected individuals, is something I really want to write about.'

In fact she started writing a novel about Africa a few years ago, but broke it off to write *Wolf Hall*. She found she was getting 'horribly spooked' by remembering her house in Africa, so she decided to give herself a day off and start *Wolf Hall*. 'And I wrote one page – and I was off! In twenty-four hours everything turned round and I couldn't keep the grin off my face – my mood had completely altered.' But she says she will reread the African novel when she has finished the *Wolf Hall* trilogy and see if she can get into it again – 'I may find it's not there for me any more. It might have gone stale on me – it might be something I have to let go. I'm not short of ideas at all – I'm just short of time to execute them.'

Her health is still problematic. 'What happened to me all those years ago has brought a LOT of complications. That was not apparent at the time. I left the hospital thinking that it was true that something cataclysmic had happened, but that I was cured. But that was far from the case.' She ballooned from a size 10 to a size 20 in a matter of months, and her thyroid eventually failed. She now also suffers from arthritis but can't take anti-inflammatory drugs because her kidneys are damaged. In 2010, she went into hospital for what was meant to be a minor bowel operation but turned into a weeks-long saga of complications and drug-induced hallucinations. But nothing ever stops her writing and even in hospital she wrote a diary, *Ink in the Blood*, which she published as a short e-book.

'I work all the time, I'm incredibly committed. I have things called holidays when I write more than I would if I were at home, but with a plane journey in between. But while the ideas are there, you've got to grasp them. That's not a complaint. I'm not saying I'm a martyr to my art – it's just a fact.' Perhaps, I suggest, she belongs in that long list of people such as Charles Darwin and Elizabeth Barrett Browning who suffered from a 'creative illness' in order to be free to work? The idea fills her with indignation: 'I'm not a romantic in that way. I just think a pain is a pain. And I cannot imagine anything in my life that would not have been better if I'd been healthy.'

She is a feminist, but I get the impression she does not like other women much. She told the *Guardian* in 2003 that she got through her schooldays by 'the simple expedient of contempt. You just decide to despise it all.' But again, she bridles when I quote it, and says she was elected head girl by the other pupils which she would not have been if she despised them. 'No. I tell you what it might have been. I have a huge contempt for women who act differently when men are around, and when I was sixteen or seventeen I did look down on girls who I knew to be sharp and clever but who changed their personality when some spotty youth hoved into view, and it may be that I was saying something like that.'

But would she accept the idea that, in her novels, she's generally kinder towards men than women? I wondered if perhaps it was because she was an older sister to two younger brothers? She concedes that there might be something in this and that many of her friends tend to be older sisters of younger brothers. 'They're very bossy! And very responsible. With younger brothers, you feel it's your job to do the worrying and make the world right for them. I always, from the moment the first one was born, loved my brothers intensely and I never saw them in any way as rivals because they were just so young. I think maybe if I am easier on men than women, that's probably the reason but to be honest, it's not because I don't like women, it's because I like men!'

But she can be very fierce towards women who annoy her (which I think by now might include me). I remember Sam Leith who was then the literary editor of the *Telegraph* telling me he was shocked by the ferocity with which she denounced an author called Judith Kelly. Kelly published a misery memoir called *Rock Me Gently* in 2005 which purported to be an account of her traumatic childhood in a Roman Catholic orphanage. Hilary Mantel went on the warpath when she read it and found that whole chunks were lifted from her novel *Fludd* and that other bits were stolen from Antonia White's *Frost in May*, and even from *Jane Eyre*. 'That was the most shocking thing. I was aghast that a book could get through without anyone recognising a passage of *Jane Eyre*. So I made a dossier – I called it my "Quarrelling Kit" – with all the passages that came from other authors. I wanted an explanation. I wanted the publishers, Bloomsbury, to stop prevaricating and pull the book. But they decided to brazen it out. The woman herself pleaded naivety – I don't think so!'

She is fierce again when I ask if she might return to Catholicism, if she might call for a priest on her deathbed? 'No. I might very well call for a Church of England vicar, but I would not call for a Catholic priest. I'm one of nature's

Protestants, Lynn; I should never have been brought up as a Catholic. I think that nowadays the Catholic Church is not an institution for respectable people.' That's quite strong – does she mean because of all the paedophile revelations? 'Yes – the fact that it could happen, the extent of the denial, the cover-up, the hypocrisy, the cruelty. When I was a child I wondered why priests and nuns were not nicer people. I thought that they were among the worst people I knew. But in a cold-blooded way, as a writer I've had full value from Catholicism – I can say that. It's a great training in doubleness – this looks like bread but it is actually a man's body, this looks like wine but it's actually blood. And that's very much a writer's way of thinking – she comes in and says good morning, but she means: Damn you to hell!'

Our lunch is over and Mantel walks painfully up the stairs to see me out. She is as she says 'a civil person' and she civilly signs my copy of *Bring Up the Bodies* and thanks me for our 'nice chat'. But I can't help wondering if she is really thinking: Damn you to hell! She wrote in her memoirs: 'My convent years left me a legacy: a nervous politeness, an appearance of feminine timidity that will probably stand me in good stead if I am ever on trial for murder.' I doubt it will come to that but don't ever make the mistake of underestimating Hilary Mantel. This animal bites.

CHAPTER ELEVEN

Artists

I'm often asked whether I choose my own subjects for interview, or whether they are chosen for me. Generally, I prefer the latter – partly because it often produces names I would never have thought of (sometimes would never have heard of) but also because it spares me the responsibility of 'backing' my choice. I can best explain this by giving an example. At some point in the early Noughties I got hooked on Meat Loaf and could never drive anywhere without playing 'Bat Out Of Hell'. (It's a particularly good song for driving to.) I loved his voice mainly, but also the fact that he was middle-aged, dishevelled, hugely overweight – i.e. not your run-of-the-mill pop star. So next time we had an ideas meeting at the *Observer* (always a rather movable feast) I said I'd like to interview Meat Loaf. A dozen startled faces turned to me, and one eventually voiced the question that was obviously hovering on all their lips, 'Why?' He didn't even have a new record out. But I spieled away about how he was such a wonderful singer, and such a fascinating man. This was my mistake.

The editor reluctantly agreed to let me interview Meat Loaf next time he was performing in London – he was not deemed worthy of an air ticket – and a meeting was eventually arranged at his hotel, the Royal Garden in Kensington. I was shocked by how old and tired he seemed – and indeed he collapsed on stage a few weeks later – but also how disagreeable. On stage and disc, he seemed to have a wonderful exuberance, but the man I met was a grumpy old codger who barely said hello before launching into a great tirade about the iniquities of British journalists and how they always get their facts wrong. As I wrote at the time, 'I expected a fearless Bat out of Hell, and found, I thought, a rather timid soul, full of worries and grumbles and actorish concerns about his "image".' I made him as interesting as I could in the article (though more by relying on his autobiography than anything he said to me) but it was uphill work, and felt vaguely dishonest. Which is why, ever since, I have been wary of 'pitching' my own choices in case I end up with another Meat Loaf.

However, having said that, there is an exception to my no-pitching rule. I am always clamouring to interview artists at any opportunity. So whenever I have built up a head of credit by interviewing half a dozen actors on the trot (editors *always* want actors, the bane of my life), I pipe up and say time for an artist now. My reasons are several. First, I don't think artists get nearly enough media coverage. They get more now than they did twenty years ago, but even so if you count the column inches devoted to, say, Lucian Freud over his entire lifetime versus the column inches devoted to, say, Victoria Beckham or even (God help us) Liz Hurley, you will find that Freud counts as practically unknown. And yet who will be of more interest in fifty years' time?

Second, I love looking at art. My husband was an artist and although I have absolutely no artistic talent myself (I managed to fail art O level) I have always enjoyed going to art galleries and exhibitions. Even in my teens, long before I met David, I would head for the Tate or the National Gallery whenever I had a free Sunday. In those days I loved the Pre-Raphaelites in the Tate and the Veroneses in the National Gallery. David had to spend years educating me and I still haven't really seen the point of Poussin – but going to galleries together became one of our strongest bonds. He would have been amazed (and rather shocked) to learn that I was a Turner Prize judge in 2006 but if I do know anything about art it is all thanks to him.

Thirdly, I like artists. It is quite rare for me to meet one I don't like. And, for interviewing purposes, I like the fact that they don't come laden with PRs – you can usually approach them directly or through their gallery and nobody sits in on the interview to make sure they don't say anything that might damage their image. Artists don't have images, thank God. And most of them drink and smoke and give good parties so being around them is fun. My only complaint is that they keep difficult hours – all their best partying is done after midnight so I have to listen to a lot of 'Oh you should have come on to Vanda's – that was a really *great* party, we didn't finish till dawn.' I wish I'd discovered art parties when I was young and able to dance all night but nowadays I am a slave to bedtime. Apparently if you take cocaine you can stay awake much longer, but I feel I'm a bit old now to embark on cocaine.

There was no question of interviewing artists when I was at the *Sunday Express* in the 1980s. Our readers were determinedly philistine and still made jokes about Picassos with two noses, or Henry Moores with holes in them. Rolf Harris was probably the only artist they approved of. But when I moved to the *Independent on Sunday* in 1990, it was possible to slip the occasional artist into the celebrity mix. I started with Gilbert and George who gave their usual fine performance and from then on I interviewed two or three artists a year, starting with the obvious ones like David Hockney, but moving on to less obvious ones like Patrick Caulfield, Gillian Ayres, Frank Stella and Robert Rauschenberg. Gillian Ayres became a good friend – but I blame her for the fact that I'm still smoking. I actually gave up for two months a few years ago, with the help of a wonder drug called Champix, but then I had lunch with Gillian at the River Café. As soon as we'd ordered our meal she said, 'Time for a fag,' and started tottering painfully (she was in her late seventies) towards the door. It was snowing so fiercely outside you couldn't see more than a yard but the waiters, obviously used to Gillian, assembled a ring of patio heaters round us, and Gillian lit up. It was not the moment to say, 'I've stopped,' so I took a cigarette and that was the end of my smoking cure.

Until the mid-1990s I interviewed a rather random selection of artists, but then the YBAs came along and seized the media's attention including mine. Damien Hirst was the first and I interviewed him (not very well) just after he won the Turner Prize. I also interviewed Rachel Whiteread and Sarah Lucas and the Chapman Brothers early in their careers, before the public knew much about them. They were all quite hard work. Jake Chapman threatened to kill me because I asked Dinos about his deformed hand. He thought it was 'rude' to discuss it – this from a man who was busy sticking phalluses on children's faces, and modelling scenes of Nazi atrocities.

I loved Sarah Lucas from the start – I wrote that 'I have never so much since school wanted to call someone my friend' – but also found her difficult because (like most artists) she refuses to explain her work. She will talk about how something is made (e.g., by frying two eggs and placing them with a kebab on a rickety old table) and even let me watch but not about its meaning. I once spent two hours watching her stick Marlboro Light cigarettes on to a blown-up yellow lifejacket. I could see it was extraordinarily painstaking work, which banished for ever the idea that her art is 'just thrown together', but when I asked why, she only murmured something about the cigarettes representing self-destruction and the lifejacket a false hope of salvation. As an interview, it lacked a certain something. But then her gallerist, lovely lovely Sadie Coles, said that Sarah was doing a show at the Cologne Art Fair and I should come over and help. I'd never been to Cologne so I thought: Why not? Sadie rang and asked me to pick up a couple of salamis at the airport. What sort? I asked. 'The size of a very big penis,' she instructed.

I arrived at the show shortly before it opened, when Sadie was unpacking shopping bags, and Sarah was busy tying two fried eggs on to a coat hanger. She said that getting the fried eggs right had been a nightmare – she'd thought the hotel chef could do them but he never got them hard enough. There was very little visible art on show – a pair of concrete boots, a sagging sofa with two pumpkins inserted at breast-height, and some beer cans stuck together to look like a penis and balls. Sarah told me that my job would be drinking lots of beer to provide more beer cans. I thought this was a bit unnecessary but then the doors opened and dozens of visitors

165

hurtled towards our stand and started queuing to buy beer-can penises at 999 D-Marks (about £330) a pop. I was astonished. I was also very quickly drunk, trying to consume enough beer to keep up with demand. Sadie had banknotes spilling out of every pocket and reckoned she took about £50,000 on the day.

In the evening, we went for dinner to the art publishers Taschen who had an enormous Jeff Koons ceramic of a child and two angels pushing a pig. It was my first glimpse of the other side of the art world – not the lonely artists in their studios, but the plutocrats who buy their stuff, the collectors. I still find them weird. I thought at one point I might like to do a book about them but Doris Saatchi, Charles Saatchi's first wife and the one who got him into art originally, took me out to lunch and told me that I would find collectors very boring indeed. It was odd, coming from her, and she didn't really explain it, but she said it so seriously I was inclined to believe her. She advised me to stick to interviewing artists, and I did.

I always feel when I'm interviewing artists that I'm doing something worthwhile. Of course some of them, like Tracey Emin or Grayson Perry, are so articulate they don't need me to get their ideas across (both of them have written superb autobiographies) but the point at which I feel I'm doing something *useful* is when I interview artists who are not natural self-publicists, and who 'don't do words'. This is what I think of as my '*pro bono*' work where, for once, my motive is not showing off as a writer but using my long experience as an interviewer to harvest information that would otherwise never be published. I remember the first time I interviewed Rachel Whiteread it was like hewing coal, trying to get the most basic biographical facts out of her, but I felt that every little nugget I collected would be of use to art historians fifty years down the line. And, as I argued to her then, I do feel that successful artists ought to talk to the media, not for reasons of self-aggrandisement, but to try to make art comprehensible to the widest possible public.

My other great mission is to find a *way* of talking about art that is not the usual repellent art bollocks. This is the jargon taught in art schools and perpetrated in art catalogues that bears no relation to English and serves only to obfuscate the subject. My favourite ever was in a catalogue at the Baltic for a Brazilian artist called Tonica Lemos Auad whose work consisted of tiny piles of carpet fluff. It read: 'Auad's carpet installations begin by the artist's delicate gathering and repositioning of minute strands of fluff, teased patiently from newly laid carpet . . . Auad sees these works as three-dimensional, site-specific drawings that create a space in which the viewer can enter and engage with the settings.' As my elder daughter pointed out, you could presumably 'engage' with the art by hoovering it up. Rather than add to the art bollocks canon, I always try to keep my artist interviews as simple as possible, asking factual questions about their childhood, their early influences, their working practices, rather than about what their art *means*. I feel that if I can supply a solid biographical background, and some account of their technique, the reader can hopefully look at the work and deduce its meaning for themselves.

My editors have generally let me choose which artists I wanted to cover and on the whole I've managed to bag the ones I wanted. The huge glaring exception was Lucian Freud who I pursued fruitlessly for years – I used to write to him once a month (my reward was a wonderfully rude handwritten letter, now framed in my loo, saying he had no wish to be 'shat on by strangers') and beg his friends to intercede on my behalf. I even got Nick Serota on board – he said he would try to persuade Freud to do an interview for his Tate show but he wouldn't. One time I was in Moro, the Spanish restaurant in Exmouth Market which was the *Observer*'s house canteen for many years, when I saw a woman who looked familiar beckoning to me across the room. But I was having lunch with my editor and felt I couldn't go table-hopping and anyway I couldn't remember the woman's name. Only when she and her companion got up to leave and walked past our table did I realise that her companion was Lucian Freud. I ran out into the street following them, but too late. A tragic missed opportunity!

As the years rolled on, I quite often found myself in the same room as Freud – he was a friend of Nicky Haslam's and I saw him at one of Nicky's birthday parties and at the great ball Nicky threw for Janet de Botton, and he would turn up sometimes to Tracey Emin's openings – but it was no good. By the end (when I think maybe he was a bit gaga) he would smile vaguely in my direction and say hello, but that was the most I ever got out of him.

I also deeply regret that I didn't interview Angus Fairhurst. I knew him from when he was Sarah Lucas's boyfriend and he was always on my wish list but I thought there was no hurry – I was working my way through the YBAs and would get to him eventually. And then he hung himself from a tree in 2008, depressed, his friends thought, by lack of recognition.

Perhaps if I'd given him a huge splash interview he wouldn't have been depressed? Perhaps it would have boosted his career at a crucial point? My interviewing career is full of these awful might-have-beens. But of course there are still zillions of artists out there I want to interview – new ones coming up, but also old ones I have been slow to see the point of.

The artist who has been my friend and guide through the art world for well over a decade is Tracey Emin. I first met her in 2001 when I interviewed her for the *Observer*, and I think maybe it was the first full-length interview she did, or the first one in which someone took her seriously. Most of her press coverage up till then had consisted of jokes about unmade beds, or photographs in *Vogue* or *Tatler* of her emerging from various parties. So although she was already famous she was still relatively unknown as a person. I was struck immediately by her honesty, her intelligence – anyone who thinks Tracey is thick must be thick themselves – and also by her commitment to her work. I have interviewed her several times since then, but this first interview is precious to me because it marks the birth of a lasting friendship.

From the *Observer*, 22 April 2001

Even in an interview, Tracey Emin wants to show you things, wants to spread her whole life out before you. Her studio in Brick Lane in London is anyway full of things to look at – the blankets she is making for her new White Cube show, the wedding dress she wears in her *Beck's Futures* film, dozens of drawings on the floor waiting for the framer's. But that is not enough for her, she wants to show you more, much more

– and she has filing cabinets full, vast archives of her life. When I asked whether her twin brother Paul looked like her ('No, he's built like a brick house. Massive'), she had to show me a photograph to prove it; when she mentions the letters she used to write telling people they could invest in her creative potential for £10, she actually digs out the file. It is as if all the time she needs proof – proof of her existence, or maybe proof that she's telling the truth?

She said we should meet at her studio in Spitalfields because her house was off-limits to journalists. But then she wanted to show me the new studio she is moving to, and somehow from there we gravitated round the corner to her house. It was surprisingly neat and smart. Naturally, I wanted to see her bed to see if it was like *My Bed*, the one Charles Saatchi bought for £150,000, but she said I couldn't because Mat (Collishaw, her boyfriend) was still asleep in it – it was five in the afternoon but they'd had a heavy night. She went to the kitchen to make tea and I was wandering rather disconsolately round the house thinking it was a bit characterless, a bit un-Tracey, until I noticed a white squidgy thing on the sofa. 'Tracey,' I squeaked, 'there's a used condom!' 'Oh dear,' she said. 'I knew I should have tidied up.'

Now truly it is strange to find a used condom lying on the sofa in an otherwise immaculate house. I even wondered if she planted it, but then decided she couldn't have because I was first into the room. What does it mean, Tracey, I nagged – was it because she couldn't bear to throw good sperm away? No, she huffed, she just hadn't got round to tidying up. But most people throw them away at the time, I told her in my new guise as expert on the nation's condom habits. 'Do they? Where?' 'Down the loo.' 'Well, I'm more the sort of person that will clean them all up in the morning. And like some people use just one condom, right? But we use tons.'

Next day, Tracey rang to say she needed to see me again. She'd had a dream in which she was a sparrow and I was a bumblebee and she was flying with one wing trying to show me something. Maybe the bed, I thought, or more details of her fascinating condom habits, but no, she wanted to meet in her local, the Golden Heart. I wondered what she could possibly show me in a pub, but the answer was waiting for me when I got there – her father, Enver Emin. He is eighty but totally compos mentis and still with a flash of the ladykiller he must once have been. But I was surprised to meet a Turkish Cypriot who looked so African. He explained that his father was jet-black – he says there were lots of Sudanese slaves in the Ottoman Empire and he thinks his family must be descended from them.

Anyway, Mr Emin was sitting placidly in the pub nursing a cup of tea, waiting to collect his wife Rose from Tracey's studio, where she was sewing blankets for Tracey's new show. I asked what he thought of Tracey's work and he said, 'I love it, but I don't understand it. She creates her own ideas, and it keeps her on her toes and keeps her happy.' He particularly likes the appliqué blankets, because they remind him of his mother. He said he was off to Cyprus on Sunday to finalise the purchase of some land to build a holiday house for Tracey and his other children. 'How many children have you got?' I asked, but when he said five, Tracey jumped on him. 'No, Dad, come on!' Apparently, he usually admits to eleven children, but he once told Tracey twenty-three – they range in age from eighteen to sixty-three. Then she started arguing with him about his having two families, and I was once more pitched into the boiling high drama that is her life (and art).

Tracey and her twin brother Paul were Enver's 'second family' in Margate. He already had a wife and family in London when he met Tracey's mother Pam, but instead of divorcing, he simply maintained two households and commuted between them. Both sides knew about each other: 'My late wife used to adore Tracey.' When the twins were four, he drove them and their mother and aunt and grandmother across Europe to Turkey, installed them in a hotel on the Black Sea, then drove back to London to collect his other family, installed them in another hotel and spent two months shuttling between them.

So it was all open and above board? Yes, he agrees, but Tracey butts in furiously: 'It was never above board, Dad! It's not above board to have two families, right?' She obviously picks this fight every time she sees him, she won't ever let things be. That is why her childhood pain is always so fresh and available to her art. If a wound shows any signs of healing, she'll pick the scab until it starts bleeding again. This is an incredible strength in her art – the way she can call up old emotions, feel old pains – but it must be quite a drawback in her life.

With other artists, such as Rachel Whiteread or Damien Hirst, you can hate the work and like the person, or vice versa, but with Tracey no such split is possible. Her art demands a sort of subservience to an Eminocentric vision of the world that feels like surrender. That is why, I think, people often resist her art for a long time and then suddenly fall for it, as Charles Saatchi did (and I did).

The best account of Tracey's life is her video *Curriculum Vitae* in Tate Modern, which is so good I don't want to spoil it. But the key facts are that she was born in Margate in 1963, and lived at first 'like a princess' – her parents ran the Hotel International and all the staff spoilt her rotten. But then the business crashed when she was seven, 'And suddenly we had nothing, and we were squatting in a cottage which used to be the staff cottage.' At that point her parents split up – she recalls her mum shouting, 'Oh go back and fuck your wife' – and from then on the little princess was just one of Margate's ordinary mob of deprived single-parent kids.

She had no front teeth (she lost them all to calcium deficiency, the result, she says, of being a twin – she has incredibly complicated bridgework now) and no boobs till she was thirteen – 'They grew really quickly. One minute I didn't have any tits and the next I had the biggest tits in the world.' At thirteen she was raped. For the next six months she avoided boys, but then she became 'a slag' – her word – and started sleeping with half the boys in Margate. 'It was a power trip, definitely. And also I had this kind of idea – why go to another country, why not just sleep with someone to get experience? In Margate, you see, underage sex was definitely the thing to do – breaking into girls. If you hadn't lost it by the time you were sixteen there was something wrong with you. It wasn't like Middle England. And also, being by the sea is brilliant because there's loads of places to have sex!'

Her film *Why I Never Became a Dancer* – one of her three favourite pieces, along with her tent and her bed – recounts her going in for a dance competition as a teenager and all the boys shouting, 'Slag, slag!' And so she resolved, 'I'm out of here, I'm better than all of you.' Despite having no O levels, she managed to get on a fashion diploma course and parlayed that into an art degree course at Maidstone. She got a first and went on to the Royal College – which she hated, but says it was her own fault for expecting too much of the college and not enough of herself.

Meanwhile, Tracey's love life was a mess. At Maidstone she had a long affair with a fellow artist, Billy Childish, which 'did her head in'. Then she had another bad affair, after the Royal College, which resulted in two abortions. Up till then she thought she couldn't get pregnant because she'd had very bad gonorrhoea as a teenager and the doctor said she would be sterile. The first abortion, in 1990, was horrendously bodged because no one realised she was carrying twins: the second abortion, she says, was 'revenge' for the first.

At this point she destroyed all her work and gave up art. 'I felt isolated, insecure, unloved, unwanted and pretty crazy, mad. I don't think I felt mad because I'd had an abortion, I think I felt mad because I was angry, and because I was living on £12 a week.' She got a job as a youth tutor for Southwark Council and took a philosophy course at Birkbeck, 'And suddenly my brain – it was like doing exercises in a gym and your muscles waking up. It was brilliant.'

But she spent two years making no art at all – it was Sarah Lucas who got her back into art. They met at Sarah's 'City Racing' show in 1992 and became instant friends. 'It was wild, brilliant, really love without sex, but totally passionate – it was almost like how girls are at school, that inseparable kind of thing.' Sarah said they should get a studio together, but Tracey said she wasn't interested in making art. OK, said Sarah, they'd get a shop and make merchandise. It was an old shop in Bethnal Green Road, and they took it for six months and called themselves the Birds and made T-shirts saying things like 'I'm so fucky'. 'What was brilliant about the shop,' Tracey recalls, 'was it gave me a platform to find what I was good at – and what I was good at was ideas, and being un-precious about them and having an audience. Sarah was very encouraging in all this.'

Then they went to Geneva together – 'our Swiss convalescence' – and made loads more stuff and Jay Jopling offered Tracey an exhibition at White Cube. 'I thought it would be my one and only exhibition so I decided to call it "My Major Retrospective". Two weeks before the show, Jay came to my tiny flat in Waterloo and apparently he left going "Omigod, what have I done", because all I could show him was this crap, smelly old ancient things like my old passport or bits of fabric from my sofa when I was three years old. There was nothing that looked like an exhibition, so Jay left thinking he'd made a big mistake.' But anyway it was a success, and four hundred people turned up for the opening.

After Sarah Lucas, her next big influence was Carl Freedman, an art curator she went out with for three years. He said if she wanted to be in his 1995 mixed show 'Minky Manky' she had to produce something big – up till then she'd only done small – and so she produced her famous tent,

Everyone I Have Ever Slept With 1963–95. Then she had a solo exhibition at the South London Gallery called 'I Need Art Like I Need God', and, 'On the opening night there were a couple of thousand people and three television crews. And I walked in and thought: Omigod, I've arrived! Her arrival was confirmed by her notorious appearance on a Channel 4 debate at the 1997 Turner Prize, pissed out of her mind and terribly funny – afterwards, she said, she didn't even know she'd been on television, she thought she was round at some boring dinner party. And then her friend Vivienne Westwood started dressing her, which gave her a whole new audience in the fashion magazines. Westwood actually doesn't think much of Emin's art (but then she doesn't like any modern art), but she admires her style. And as Tracey says, the collaboration works to their mutual advantage, 'It's symbiotic. And it's fantastic for a woman of my age, thirty-seven, to be like this muse and this glamour thing – we're having fun with it.'

In 1999, Tracey hogged all the publicity for the Turner Prize with her notorious *My Bed*, and then didn't win. She thinks it was a plot, she thinks the Tate just used her for publicity and never seriously considered giving her the prize. She is quite bitter about it, still. When I said I'd forgotten who did win, she crowed, 'Exactly! People don't remember – it was Steve McQueen. But all the papers had my photograph, not his. Revenge is sweet.' She forced herself to keep smiling at the time, but she cried bitterly afterwards. And she blames that disappointment for the kidney infection that put her in hospital a few months later. Her health has always been precarious – one of the first things she did when she started making money was to take out private health insurance. 'I'm sickly and I get run down and I have very bad herpes, and I like knowing that the doctor's there.'

Of course, in the past, her sickliness was exacerbated by her non-stop drinking, progressing from beer to wine to brandy through the day. 'When I went out, I had a brilliant bag that could hold four beers, half a bottle of brandy and cigarettes all the way round, and also I was sponsored by Bombay Sapphire Gin, so I used to always take a bottle of gin as well. And even when I didn't go out, I'd be sitting round drinking.' Why this abuse? 'I don't think it was abuse. It was more like rock 'n' roll!' she cackles. Her drinking got so bad about three years ago, she had constant diarrhoea and her weight went down to six and a half stone. She also got really boringly aggressive at parties, till finally Mat and her friends said pack it in or they'd leave her. So in September 1999, she gave up spirits – she still drinks wine and gets pissed at parties, but not to the same annihilating degree.

Nowadays, she says, she looks after herself – she goes to the gym and is learning to box. And she has a good solid relationship with her fellow artist Mat Collishaw, now in its fourth year. Moreover, she is faithful – 'But of course I think probably no one else is!' She and Mat could afford to have children but she says she's too old and also, 'We have a really good life, we like it the way it is. If I keep fit and healthy, and in shape, I do actually have a few good years.'

But clearly the question of having children is preying on her mind – she's just made a film with her mother which is 'basically me asking her why she won't let me have children. My mum has never wanted me to have children. She thinks I would be destroying my life, even now. I asked is it because she thinks I'm so mentally unstable she'd be frightened for me and she said, "Yes, that's one of the reasons." The fact that I've got over so much, she wouldn't want anything to come into my life that would make me fragile again.'

How fragile is she? She seems cheerful and robust at present, but she has had plenty of brushes with madness in the past and at least one suicide attempt, when she threw herself off a cliff, aged twenty – 'But I'm a really good swimmer!' There was another very bad patch around her abortion in 1990, and one three years ago – perhaps the period of self-neglect commemorated in *My Bed*. When she goes down, she says, it's like a spiral in which one failure reminds her of every other failure in her life – that's why she could never face taking her driving test, because if she failed it would be like failing to win the Turner Prize and every other failure before that. But now she is determined to take her driving test and keep on taking it till she passes.

At least now she seems to have got out of the habit of destructive relationships that was such a feature of her teens and twenties. In those days, she says, she was so nihilistic she thought: I am shit, and that is why I am treated like shit. Was success as good as she expected? 'Better! I'm happier. I look after myself more. I'm kinder to myself. I've got a nice house. And if I didn't want to work for a couple of years I wouldn't have to – it's a great feeling, to know I'm doing it because I want to do it. The downside is I get terrible stress and my mind goes blank and I lose concentration because there are people on my case all the time for all kinds of shit. People try constantly to use me and I hate it.'

I must say that her life, what I saw of it, is incredibly

pressured. The phone in her studio rings non-stop, and although she has a brilliant PA, Gemma, she has to keep making decisions. While I was there, she was having a great row with the ICA about the 'Beck's Futures' exhibition because they were planning to show her new film in the bar and she wanted it in the cinema. She told Gemma to relay the news that she wouldn't be attending the opening party after all – and suddenly the director of the ICA was on the phone grovelling, saying of course she could have the cinema. 'The wheel that squeaks gets the oil!' she crowed as she put the phone down.

I was amazed to see that a fortnight before her White Cube opening, half the work was still incomplete. Her step-mother was busy sewing the blankets, her assistant was building the 17-foot tower, *Helter Skelter*, which will be the centrepiece of the show, but she hadn't even started the four paintings she had promised to make. All this, I'd have thought, was panic enough, but she had also agreed to appear on *Have I Got News for You* and said she ought to try and read the newspapers – though her main prepara-tion would be choosing her lowest décolletage to frighten Ian Hislop.

She is also supposed to be writing a novel – she says it will have to be a novel rather than an autobiography because 'one thing that success has taught me is censorship'. But why does she want to write? Are there things she can't say in her art? 'Yes, because – I should be careful what I say here, but I don't think I'm visually the best artist in the world, right? I've got to be honest about this. But when it comes to words, I have a uniqueness that I find almost impossible in terms of art – and it's my words that actually make my art quite unique.'

Aha! This used to be my own theory about Tracey, that she was a great writer and a merely so-so artist. If you see her drawings or her blankets from a distance, without reading the words, you think 'pretty' but not much more. It is the words that give them their edge. That is why *My Bed* was such a breakthrough, because it didn't rely on words – but I suspect it relied on our knowing stuff about her history that we only knew from her previous words. But I've now revised my theory because there is a piece of hers in the Tate that is only words, *For Joseph Samuels, 1981*, and although it is vividly written, it is pretty tame by her standards. So she needs both – the fierceness of the words playing off the delicacy of the art – to really make her point.

Finally, I asked about this habit of hoarding things, the way she keeps archives of her life, never lets the past go. 'Perhaps it's because I never grew up.' Or is it because she needs proof – as a teenager, did people call her a liar? 'Yes. And not just as a teenage girl but even as a woman. That's a good theory, I like that. And maybe I don't believe things myself, as well. Truth is such a transient thing . . . it's like with my work, people say, "Oh, the honesty and the truth behind it" – but it's all edited, it's all calculated, it's all decided. I decide to show this or that part of the truth, which isn't necessarily the whole story, it's just what I decide to give you.' So with this interview – honest as far as it goes, I hope, but only a fragment of the whole Tracey.

*

That was my first encounter with Tracey and we got on well but I didn't really expect to see her again. But, very much to my surprise, she kept inviting me to lunches and parties and openings and seemed to want to be friends. She mainly talked about herself and I thought that her idea of friendship was a bit of a one-way street, but then she was incredibly kind when my husband died in 2003 and kept ringing up to see if I was all right. She thought I was becoming agoraphobic (I wasn't, but I wasn't socialising) and insisted that I come to a party at the National Portrait Gallery with her. So that was kind, and she was even more kind a few years later when my little cat Delilah died of cancer. I rang my daughters to wail, 'Boo hoo, boo hoo, I had to have Delilah put down!' and they were mildly sympathetic but only mildly. 'You can easily get another cat,' said one, and, 'Well you've still got Samson,' said the other – both a bit brisk for my taste. I was still wailing when Tracey rang so I told her my cat just died and of course, as the mother of Docket and a besotted cat-lover, she understood my grief immediately, listened patiently to my outpourings, and sent a shedload of flowers.

I saw her at the 2005 Venice Biennale (when Gilbert and George represented Britain) and Tracey said wistfully that she'd love to do a Biennale, but she didn't think the British Council would ever choose her. But lo and behold, she was chosen for the very next Biennale in 2007 so I persuaded the *Observer* to let me cover the story at length, from all the months of preparation to the opening. This was the nearest I ever got to seeing Tracey at work and I was struck time and again by her perfectionism. She actually paid for the restoration of the British pavilion, she was so eager to get everything right. 'Doing the Biennale' with Tracey was probably the most glamorous week of my life – night after night of dinners in gorgeous restaurants, parties in fabulous palazzi, whizzing between them in Ronnie Wood's private launch. Unfortunately Tracey herself did not enjoy the Biennale, partly because she was ill, partly because she was having rows with her boyfriend, and also because her show was roundly panned by the British press (though not by the international press). Afterwards, she told me, she cried for a week.

But then, being Tracey, she bounced back, with highly praised shows in Edinburgh and at the Hayward Gallery and a very interesting show in which she 'embellished' some gouaches Louise Bourgeois gave her shortly before she died. She has regular shows in Rome, New York and London but has recently branched out into South America, and Miami. She celebrated her fiftieth birthday last year with a great party for all her friends at her house near St Tropez, and a visit to Château La Coste where she unveiled a new outdoor sculpture, followed by a party on the beach where, oddly, Joan Collins turned up. Tracey does have some very unexpected friends. I am lucky to be one of them.

CHAPTER TWELVE

On Being Interviewed

Obviously being interviewed is pretty odd if you're used to doing the interviewing yourself. As an interviewer, my aim is always to talk as little as possible – ideally I want a one-sentence question to yield a three-paragraph answer – and I'm confused at having to yack away about myself. I suppose it's what one dreams of as a teenager – meeting a man who says, 'Tell me all about yourself, you fascinating creature!' But ever since my teenage fiasco with a conman I've been a bit guarded. I can only open up when I know I can trust someone, and I very rarely trust anyone I'm meeting for the first time. Perhaps especially journalists.

My big dose of being interviewed happened in 2009 when I published my memoir *An Education*, and when the film based on my conman experience came out. But actually I had some experience of being interviewed before that – I'd 'done publicity' for my two sex books and two collections of interviews (*Mostly Men* and *Demon Barber*) and generally took the line that if publishers or employers asked me to chat to the media I should oblige. It does not behove journalists to say they are shy.

But some of those early interviews were very odd. I remember a particularly strange radio interview with Michael

Parkinson about my first collection, *Mostly Men*. He was in something of a career trough at the time, no longer on the telly but doing radio interviews with nobodies like me. And it was obvious from the moment I walked into the studio that he hated me. Almost his first words were, 'You know Melvyn Bragg is a good friend of mine?' Uh huh.

One of the interviews reproduced in *Mostly Men* was with Melvyn Bragg and it was not flattering. It was published in one of the first issues of the *Independent on Sunday* in 1990, and apparently Melvyn Bragg practically had a breakdown when he read it – it seems nobody had ever said a harsh word about him before. My harsh words were to the effect that he wasted a lot of time on *The South Bank Show* showing reaction shots of himself looking pensive or grinning, when he could just be concentrating on the interviewee.

Bragg retaliated by putting a hideously ugly woman interviewer into his next trashy novel, and now Parky was trying to add his mite by giving me a radio grilling. But he chose an odd tack. He decided to 'expose' the fact that I had once worked for *Penthouse*. It wasn't much of an exposure given that I'd said it in the author blurb of my book, but his line was: How could I call myself a feminist if I'd worked for *Penthouse*? I'm not sure that I ever did 'call myself' a feminist. I mean obviously I was and am a feminist, being a woman and all, but I've never particularly *called* myself one. But Parky wouldn't let it go. He spent the entire interview telling me off for working for *Penthouse*, and confirmed what I already thought anyway: that he was an exceptionally dull interviewer.

As well as professional interviews, I also gave dozens of interviews to students from my husband's media studies course at the Central London Polytechnic. I gave an annual lecture on interviewing and said that if anyone fancied interviewing a celeb, I would be happy to critique the result. They had to find the celeb themselves, and some of them did, but a few had the bright idea of asking if they could interview me instead. I always said yes, on condition that they sent me the finished article to appraise. I gave them a one-hour time slot, say from 4.15 to 5.15, which I regarded as their first test. Could they turn up on time? And could they accept that an hour meant an hour? Of course most of them turned up late and then looked surprised when I said, 'Well it's 5.15 now, your time's up.' They probably thought I was a real grouchy cow – which I was – but I wanted to inculcate the lesson that punctuality *matters* in journalism. An article that is late for its deadline will probably never be published at all. And if you have sometimes spent days negotiating with a PR about whether you will have sixty or seventy-five minutes with an interviewee, as I have done, you know it would be daft to waste any one of those minutes by turning up late.

I learned a lot from letting students interview me. But what I mainly learned was that I could never tell during the interview how good they were. Some students seemed really on the ball, asked interesting questions, elicited interesting answers – and then went away and wrote a completely standard piece with no insight at all. I advised such students to head for television or radio – they were good at interviewing, they just weren't any good at writing it up. It was the other type who interested me, the ones who seemed rather bumbling and inattentive at the time, and then came back with a humdinger of a piece full of sharp observations on my voice, my smoking, my 'tinkly' laugh, my way of dealing with awkward questions ('I can't remember' my usual standby), but also noticing their surroundings, my drawing room, my cat. I was often amazed that someone who had seemed half-asleep could have picked up so much good detail.

So, as I say, I was not a complete novice when I started doing publicity for *An Education* in 2009. But I found the whole experience unexpectedly intense because suddenly there were dozens of interviews to do, not just for the UK, but also for Ireland, Australia, New Zealand, and then endless 'down-the-lines' for regional radio stations. And I was quite nervous about doing them because I was always afraid of letting slip the real name of my conman, which I wanted to keep secret. I'd called him 'Simon' in the book and then Nick Hornby, who wrote the screenplay, changed his name to 'David' in the film – which was confusing because it was also the name of my husband – so I always did a mental double-take when anyone asked about 'David'.

There was also the problem of my parents. I knew they wouldn't see the film (my father being blind, my mother crippled with arthritis, both in their nineties) but I thought that other people in their retirement home might come across my interviews – as indeed they did. Almost every interviewer attacked me for being 'cruel' to my parents. I would say unsentimental rather than cruel – or perhaps unsparing would be a better word. With friends and daughters I could defend myself by saying, 'But look, you *know* what monsters my parents are!' and anyone who had experienced my father's shouting and my mother's wilful obtuseness would warmly agree. But I couldn't say that to the public at large because I knew there would be a keen audience at Bramble Cottage retirement home. So I really had to just take it on the chin – which is something you learn to do a lot in interviews.

(I remember when interviewing Vanessa Redgrave, I quoted a paragraph from her autobiography where one of her children said wistfully, 'Can't you stay with us, Mummy? Do you *have* to go and save all these other people?' It seemed to me a crucial admission – that Redgrave was so busy saving the world, she neglected her own daughters – and I said accusingly, 'Don't you regret that?' 'Yes,' she said simply, 'I do.' All my huffy-puffy moral indignation deflated instantly, and I found myself murmuring, 'Oh well, we've all made mistakes.' It was the honesty and genuine regret that was disarming.)

Anyway I did the first round of interviews for my book in early summer 2009, but knew I had to do another round in the autumn because the book was coming out in Australia and New Zealand, closely followed by the film. My mother fell ill in July and I spent a lot of time visiting her in Brighton Hospital but she seemed to be on the mend so I went for my usual week's holiday in France. She died the day after I got back. She was ninety-two, she'd been in hospital with breathing difficulties and was told she had a dicky heart – I should not have been as surprised as I was. Nevertheless I was in a fog of disbelief for weeks: My mother *died* – how could that be? I always thought she would outlive me.

I was still puzzling this over when I had to do my next radio interview, a 'down-the-line' from a London studio to an Irish station. The interviewer asked something about my parents, and I was chatting about them, getting into a by now familiar groove, when I suddenly thought: Hang on. My mother's dead. But the interviewer had moved on to ask about something else, and I thought: This is not the moment to say, 'By the way, my mother died.' And after that – after that one lie by omission – I decided not to tell any interviewers my mother died because if I told one, then I'd have to tell them all and I didn't feel ready to talk about it yet. So I went on talking about my parents as if they were both still alive, right through the film premiere and into the New Year. I didn't finally tackle the subject until my father died a few months later, when I wrote an article about becoming an orphan for the *Sunday Times*. I preferred to write it in my own words, rather than try to explain my very complex mix of feelings (guilt, relief, sorrow) to an interviewer. But it meant that for more than six months I kept up this strange lie.

My father died in May and very soon afterwards I was asked to do *Desert Island Discs* with Kirsty Young. Naturally, I was thrilled and wished my parents could have been alive to hear it. I included a favourite song of my father's, 'Abdul Abulbul Amir', as one of my eight records and was touched afterwards to get dozens of letters from old people saying they hadn't heard the song for decades and were so glad to hear it again – they thought nobody else remembered it.

I knew that Kirsty Young was a good interviewer (much better than Sue Lawley) because I'd been listening to *Desert Island Discs* for ever, but it was only when she interviewed me that I realised how very, very good she is. I'd thought that all her questions would be pre-planned, and of course many of them were, but she also made impromptu connections that couldn't have been scripted. For instance, I chose Pulp's

'Common People' as my first record and she asked if I would call myself a friend of Jarvis Cocker's and I said no, I'd met him a few times and obviously admired him but not enough to count as a friend, and then she used that as a link to ask about my friendship with Tracey Emin. Time and again she made these deft segues, and I was dazzled by her speed of thought.

But she also asked some quite hostile questions. She picked up the admission in my book that I'd been very promiscuous at Oxford (of course I knew she would) and nagged away at it like a terrier with a bone. 'You say you slept with fifty men! In two terms! And those terms aren't very long, are they?' No, I agreed limply, I was rather jamming them in. This unfortunate turn of phrase was of course much relished by the tabloids who quoted it endlessly. Come to think of it, perhaps it was just as well my parents were dead.

Another thought. My daughters were already in their thirties when this publicity blitz happened, and I knew I didn't have to worry about upsetting them. They had heard all my shocking revelations before and joked about them with their friends. I had taken the precaution, when I wrote *An Education*, of showing them the manuscript before I sent it to the publisher, in case I'd said anything that might upset them, but they gave it the green light. But supposing I'd been doing all these interviews years earlier while my daughters were still at school? I would have had to censor myself – though how well I would have succeeded is doubtful. But it gave me more sympathy with interviewees who have children at home, who must always have to think about how their remarks will go down at their children's school.

As well as doing interviews about *An Education*, I also started being invited to talk at book festivals, which was a whole new world to me. Of course they were fun, but I am still puzzled by the idea that people will pay to hear writers *talking*, when the whole pleasure of books for me is that they don't require a captive audience in a hall but just one person reading privately in an armchair. Poets are different of course – I can understand why they would want to read their poetry aloud and other people would want to listen to them. But I couldn't face reading my own prose out loud and said that, rather than give readings, I would prefer to be interviewed on stage and take questions from the audience.

I said yes almost indiscriminately to all the festivals that asked me. One of them was Richmond, which I happily accepted because Richmond is only a couple of miles from Twickenham where I grew up. The date was in my diary, the arrangements were made, and then they asked me to send an author photo for their programme. I sent my favourite photo, taken by Johnnie Shand Kydd, which showed me wreathed in smoke, enjoying a cigarette. The organisers said they couldn't use it! They had funding from Richmond Council and health and safety regulations meant they were not allowed to publish anything that promoted smoking. Could I send them another photograph? No, I said. If the good burghers of Richmond were going to be so terrorised by a photograph of me smoking, imagine what my actual presence would do! The organiser was very sweet and kept offering compromises, but I withdrew on principle and Richmond had to struggle along without me.

Publishers like sending you to book festivals because, hope-fully, you sell lots of books by signing them afterwards. And it was always gratifying to see a queue of people holding copies of *An Education*, waiting patiently for me to sign them. But one of the curiosities of these book-signings was that, more often than not, I would notice some woman, often about my own age or slightly younger, hanging around the back of the queue because she wanted to talk to me afterwards. One or two of these women had been to Lady Eleanor Holles and wanted to ask if I remembered so-and-so (I never did – I am hopeless on names) but, more interestingly, a few of them had memories of Simon, my conman. One of them had been 'engaged' to him and had a daughter by him but of course he did a bunk immediately. Another woman my own age told me that her daughter had gone out with an illegitimate son of Simon's who went to Israel to look for him when he was eight-een. He found Simon eventually, but it was not a happy meet-ing, and he came back rather appalled by what he had seen of his father.

Perhaps this is a good opportunity to finish the story of Simon. When *An Education* came out, he rang me a couple of times from Israel but I always slammed the phone down as soon as I heard his voice. The *Daily Mail* offered to fly me out to Israel to meet him – they said they'd tracked him down through various aliases though none of the names meant anything to me – along with a reporter. I can't think of anything I'd like less. To meet Simon again would be bad enough, but with a *Mail* reporter present! People kept asking, 'Aren't you curious to meet him?' But no, absolutely not. He would tell a pack of lies about his life's adventures, claiming he had always loved me, and I would look at him and think: How disgusting that I ever imagined I could marry such a lying slimeball.

Anyway, I learned in early 2013 that he was dead. I had an email from a man in Israel who said he believed I knew his late father, and enclosing some photos that were obviously of Simon. He said he wanted to talk to me about his father in order to 'move on' with his life. I had no desire to talk to him, but I wanted confirmation that Simon was dead, and I remembered that one of the women I'd met at a book festival had said she knew a son of Simon's (a different son – he seems to have had zillions of children) who lived in Glasgow. Eventually I tracked her down and she confirmed that yes, Simon had died about a year earlier. Phew! I was amazed at how relieved I was, that I would never hear his creepy voice on the phone again. Everyone tells me I should forgive him, but why? He took advantage of my youth, but much worse was the way he so coolly conned my parents. He knew that he had to get them on side and he set about it in a very calculated manner, flattering my mother about her looks and my father about his intelligence. And they were so ashamed afterwards they wouldn't even mention Simon's name until a few months before they died. When my mother said 'Forgive me' on her deathbed, I think it was for Simon she meant.

When paedophilia became a hot topic in the early Noughties, I heard the term 'grooming' for the first time and recognised immediately that that was what Simon did to my parents. Technically, he was not a paedophile because I was sixteen when I met him, but sixteen-year-olds were more innocent then, and it was essentially a paedophile relationship. My whole appeal to him was that I was a schoolgirl, and his to me was that he was a grown-up, and he relied on the fact that schoolgirls didn't question what grown-ups did.

But I hadn't really defined this thought until I went to watch the filming of *An Education* at the old Haberdashers' Aske's school in Ealing. Carey Mulligan and the other girls were acting a classroom scene with their teacher, played by Olivia Williams, and when the scene ended Olivia Williams rushed up saying she had lots of questions she wanted to ask me. Most of her questions were about my memories of school, but then she asked, 'Do you think he was a paedophile?' And without a second's thought I answered yes. Amanda Posey, the co-producer of the film, almost fainted. Apparently this had been a huge problem all the time her husband Nick Hornby was writing the script – *on no account* must Simon be seen as a paedophile, because then no good actor would agree to play him and audiences would stay away in droves. So thanks to Nick's script, and the brilliant casting of Peter Sarsgaard, they managed to fudge the age question in the film, and I'd just airily blown it. Amanda presumably swore Olivia Williams to secrecy and tactfully suggested to me that if ever asked the question again, I should perhaps rethink my answer. But anyway, yes, I believe he was a paedophile and that he groomed my parents to deliver me to him, and that is why I have never felt the slightest desire to forgive him.

An Education gave me my first glimmer of what it must be like to be famous. Until then, I'd believed that I was entirely a private person. Other journalists probably knew who I was, but I was not a figure of public interest. But then, through the book and, even more, the film, people I didn't know seemed to know about *me*, which I found disconcerting. Often they addressed me as if we were old friends so I'd be racking my brain the whole time thinking: Who is this person? and feeling guilty about my bad memory. It must be a million times worse for really famous people when everyone they meet seems to know them. It gives me a bit more sympathy with my interviewees than perhaps I had before.

CHAPTER THIRTEEN

Age

I'm writing this on my sixty-ninth birthday so the question of age looms large. Next year it will be three score years and ten which I've always believed, and still believe, is quite enough. I suffered from having parents who lived to ninety-two and wouldn't wish the same on my own children. But I'll have to have a seventieth birthday party! And see this book published! Maybe I'll stick around a bit longer, or lie about my age.

Not that lying about my age will fool anyone. I have a friend, same age as me, who gets terribly hurt if she *isn't* asked for proof of her age when she requests a senior concession at the cinema. I'm always amazed if they do. I know I look old because three times recently people have offered to help me with my luggage on the train. The first two were men – foreigners of course – but the last when I was coming back from a party in Hastings, and maybe looking a bit extra shaky from a hangover, was a woman, and not a young woman either, but a woman of about fifty with bleached blonde hair and tattoos. And although I declined her kind offer, and said I was fine, thank you, I realised I must look very old indeed and I could either cry about it or decide: I don't mind and thank God there are still a few people – not many – who feel inclined to help old people with their luggage. I suppose someone soon will want me to do an oral history about how it felt to grow up in the dark ages of the 1950s without a television or computer, and did we have gas lighting and keep coal in the bath? But OK, I'm up for it, I'll do old if that's what's required and I certainly don't want to pretend to be young.

It strikes me that there are two basic stereotypes for women my age and older. You can either be a sweet old biddy, patting kiddies on the head and saying how you long to put your feet up and have a nice cup of tea. Or you can be a wicked witch who scares people stiff. I'll go for the latter. I already own a black cat, and sometimes talk to it; I could easily advance to muttering in the street, and waving a walking stick at irritating children. Basically it's a choice between do I want to be feared or do I want to be patronised and frankly I prefer the former. My father managed to terrify people even when he was ninety and blind, which I found admirable. It required a lot of shouting, though, which I'm not very good at.

Sixty-nine is pretty old for a journalist – of course it's pretty old for anyone, but particularly for someone in what is supposedly (though not really) a young profession. In my thirties I assumed I would retire at sixty, but when I got to sixty I was still enjoying work, so there seemed no good reason to stop. Also, I was newly widowed and desperately needed work to distract me, to get me out of the house. Maybe I should warn my employers that I will never voluntarily retire. They will have to prise my gnarled fingers from the keyboard and I will kick up an almighty fuss. That is assuming newspapers still exist by then.

I'm probably the oldest still-practising interviewer, which is quite an odd thing to be. Whenever interview scenes are portrayed in television drama or films, they usually consist of a young, pretty woman interviewing an older man. And of course that's how it was when I started. Interviewing was seen as a form of flirtation; it was assumed that a younger woman could winkle out secrets merely by batting her eyelashes. Actually, I don't think I ever flirted with my interviewees, but I suppose I capitalised on the fact that I *was* young, and pretty. Quite likely I giggled a lot, and crossed and uncrossed my legs a few times – I had *fabulous* legs in those days, I once came third in a national Lady Cantrece Lovely Legs competition (Lady Cantrece was a brand of tights) – so it is not impossible that some of my interviewees fancied me. But I was already in love with David, so I certainly never went on a date with an interviewee.

When I started, my interviewees were always older than me, and nearly always men, and it felt very natural (probably because of my relationship with my father) to be asking cheeky questions of an older man. I was much more inhibited about interviewing women. If they were great beauties, or famous actresses, I felt in awe of them; if they were not beauties – if they were writers for instance! – I felt that my own prettiness put me at a disadvantage and that they were bound to hate me. The upshot was I avoided interviewing women as much as possible.

But in my late twenties I suddenly came up against the question of age. As I mentioned before, the *Evening Standard* commissioned me to do a series of interviews with footballers and it came as a terrible shock one day to realise that I was interviewing someone younger than me. The footballer was maybe twenty-five to my twenty-nine but it still felt obscurely wrong, humiliating. On the one hand, he was thick as two planks, but on the other he was married, with two children, and owned a substantial house. He felt like a grown-up, albeit a stupid one, whereas I still felt like a student. I thought: Is this what my life is going to be from now on, trying to wring a few interesting remarks from morons who are younger than me? If someone had told me then that I would be interviewing a tennis player (Rafa Nadal) when I was old enough to be his grandmother, I might have packed up my career there and then. Luckily, my footballer series didn't last long, but it was the first hint of something that would become a problem later on.

Apart from the footballers, nearly all the people I interviewed in my twenties and thirties were older than me, which was fine. But when I was at the *Independent on Sunday* in my mid-forties, it occurred to me that, if I only interviewed older people, this would be an ever-diminishing field and probably quite a boring one. If I wanted to stay current, if I wanted to be a contender (which I did), I would have to interview younger people. I found it hard at first. I remember going to Jonathan Ross's gorgeous house overlooking Hampstead Heath and thinking: It's not fair. I could accept that pop stars and film stars became very rich very young but to find someone who was 'only' a television presenter (sorry, Wossy) living in such glamour was quite a shock. (I'm often asked if I ever envy the people I interview and I can answer truthfully no. But I do sometimes envy their houses.)

Luckily this dilemma eased when I left the *Independent on Sunday* to join *Vanity Fair* and they only ever asked me to interview older people. But in fact they very rarely asked me to interview anyone at all. This led to another dilemma. I was under exclusive contract to *Vanity Fair* which meant I was not allowed to write for anyone else, but they only gave me half a dozen interviews in two years. I was fabulously well paid but I was stuck at home twiddling my thumbs. I suppose in retrospect I should have learned to play the piano or something, but I mainly spent my time reading British press interviews and grinding my teeth that it wasn't me doing them. A whole new crop of interviewers – Ginny Dougary, Jan Moir, Deborah Ross – had arrived to steal my thunder. So by the time *Vanity Fair* dropped my contract, I was so hungry for interviews I would have interviewed children, cats, dogs, footballers, anyone, and my qualms about younger people had disappeared.

My preference now, in old age, is to interview *much* younger people – so much so that I get a bit sniffy if anyone offers me Sir David Attenborough or Diana Athill. I feel I've done old people: I know a lot of them as friends and I am one myself. Whereas young people are a whole new world. Often I don't know what they're talking about but they're quite pleased and amused when I ask them to explain. It reminds them of talking to their grannies. I still feel a bit goatish asking young people about their sex lives but it's much easier now than when I was in my forties – they know I have no evil designs on them and they are often surprisingly frank. I think there are advantages for the reader too.

The trouble with young interviewers is that they're wet behind the ears. They believe what PRs tell them! They are thrilled if a record company flies them out to Croatia to watch a British group perform. They don't ever wonder why they couldn't have watched the group in England (answer – because they might not seem so exciting in a half-full hall in Paignton). They are grateful for the free T-shirts PRs give them – especially nowadays when they are so badly paid they probably need all the free clothing they can get. They don't ask why a film has been 'in the pipeline' for three years (answer – because it is so bad it will go straight to DVD) or why an actor has not been seen on screen for over a decade (numerous answers – but often because he's become uninsurable either through drink, drugs or general seediness). Journalists are often told off for being cynical. They don't have to be cynical but they do *always* have to be sceptical, and this is harder for the young.

The young don't have that automatic bullshit detector which I think only comes with age. If they meet someone who says he's a successful entrepreneur they believe him without even asking any back-up questions (What is your company called? What does it do? Can I look it up in Companies House? Are you in the *Sunday Times* Rich List?). That is why it's so easy for conmen to con people. If someone is supposed to be rich it should be possible to establish how they made their money, otherwise alarm bells should ring. This was a lesson I learned the hard way from Simon.

There's a type of person – the opposite of bullshit artists – who I'm intrigued by. They are people who *never* advertise what they do, who never boast, who can enter a room or a restaurant without drawing attention to themselves and would never in a million years say, 'Do you know who I am?' But there's a quiet confidence about them that I have learned to recognise over the years. They know that the people who matter know that they matter, and they have no interest in impressing the others. Unfortunately such people rarely give interviews. But they're the ones I've learned to look out for.

The interviews that most often fail, I feel, are those between young, childless interviewers and older subjects with children. The young never understand what a difference parenthood makes. Thus they can blithely write that someone 'flits between homes' in London, New York, Los Angeles without ever asking the obvious question – Yes, but where do the children go to school? Once you have children, you have to be anchored somewhere, you have to have a base. In general, young interviewers never seem to ask enough questions about family – not just children but aged parents. They tend to believe that career is all. But even stars, however mad and self-obsessed, do actually have family commitments – or if they don't, I assume they have psychological problems. Young interviewers only want to know about the glamorous bits of their lives but I'm much more interested in the unglamorous stuff – what they do if they're alone in a hotel room; who, if anyone, they phone with good news or bad; how often they speak to their mums.

So I think being old is quite useful for an interviewer. But there is nothing else good about it. I suppose I slightly prefer my sixties to my fifties in that there is none of that pressure to stay young and 'not let yourself go'. I was always dying to let myself go, to stop pretending to be younger or fitter than I was. There was a particularly nasty patch in my fifties when friends were always recommending HRT. I never considered it for a moment: I'm far too frightened of drugs. Also I noticed, but didn't like to say, that it made my friends mad. Luckily, they've all calmed down again now.

I suppose I could pretend there is a sort of wisdom in age. Is there? I certainly didn't see it in my parents, and I don't think my daughters see it in me. I have a bit more knowledge of how the world works but am still shockingly naïve in many ways. I wish I understood economics, or business, or anything to do with money. I reckon I am quite a good judge of people, but how does one ever know? And I remember how impatient I was, when young, with the supposed wisdom of older people. I just thought: You dinosaurs, don't you realise that the world has moved on?

I'm guiltily aware that I had the best of it, that I enjoyed the golden age of interviewing. I came along at just the right time, the 1980s, when newspapers were suddenly keen to have their own star interviewers, and when it was still possible to spend enough time with celebs to make the interviews worth reading. But that is hardly the case now. My friend Deborah Ross recently had to fly to New York to interview Bruce Willis for *The Times*. She had just fourteen minutes with him which she worked out (clever girl!) meant she flew 600 miles for every minute of interview time, and then had to produce 3,000 words in two days. I couldn't have done that even when young, and I certainly couldn't begin to do it now.

I was lucky that I started in a seller's market so I was able to set my own rules. I wouldn't agree to interview anyone unless I had at least ninety minutes with them. I needed two days to prepare and at least a week to write the piece. I would never do phone interviews. I would never willingly jump on a plane unless there was a really thrilling interviewee at the end of it. Someone in the office, not me, would have to make all the arrangements and deal with PRs. No word of my copy – or punctuation – could be changed without my permission. And I had a right of veto over whom I was willing to interview.

I still get away with most of those demands, but only, I think, by virtue of my great age. If I were starting my career now, and tried to insist that I wouldn't do phone interviews and wouldn't let anyone change my copy, editors would laugh in my face. Rightly, perhaps. But *someone* has to set some standards, and editors won't. If you treat interviewers like junior reporters, if you expect them to dash off to a film publicity circus with no preparation, interview an actor for fifteen minutes and write a 2,000-word piece the same day, is it any wonder that readers start complaining that interviews are boring?

CHAPTER FOURTEEN

What I've Learned

What have I learned from doing all these hundreds of interviews? Not much, you might say. But I've certainly come a long way since Twickenham. I retain my core belief that other people are essentially unknowable – that however well you *think* you know them there are always undercurrents you will never understand. I only learned when my husband was dying that he had always believed (wrongly) that he was not his brothers' brother. That's a pretty big discovery to make after thirty years of marriage.

Going out with a conman in my teens taught me not to take people at face value, and not always to believe everything they say. My conman announced his engagement to me and celebrated with my parents while he was living with a wife and children half a mile down the road. That experience scarred me for life. Once you have had an early lesson in distrust, it is very difficult to unlearn it. I wish I could. The habit of distrust, or scepticism, has been useful to me as a journalist, but I would be a much nicer person without it.

Muriel Spark believed that many people lead double lives – she often used the expression 'living a lie' – and this was something that was confirmed at *Penthouse*. We used to get dozens of letters from men – often on expensive stationery

– saying that they had to have a bit of bondage now and again, or a quickie with a rent boy on the way home from work. Apparently much of it went on around Pimlico – so convenient for commuters from Victoria. Their wives would never know. And sometimes elderly, distinguished-looking gentlemen would come to the office asking for the phone number of the Pet of the Month, saying they thought she was their long-lost niece. They might pick up some Penteez Panties while they were about it. There was a brothel – a pink bungalow called I think the Love Cottage – quite near *Penthouse* in Baron's Court, and I once interviewed the madam there who kept me in stitches for hours with her stories of judges and MPs, and their need to be told they were naughty boys. Consequently, whenever some pinstriped pillar of society is droning on, I can't help wondering: What's your kink? At least it keeps me amused.

Thinking that other people are unknowable might seem like a handicap in an interviewer but I believe it's an advantage. It means I always feel there's more to discover, more to understand, more to be curious about. I don't take anything for granted. And I've learned what again should have been obvious – that other people are very different from me, and very different from each other. I find this reassuring. I want there to be the widest possible variety of individuals in the world. I would hate everyone to be the same and I loathe the media tendency to lump people into types or classes or stereotypes – northerners versus southerners, middle-class versus working-class, introverts versus extraverts. One I'm particularly infuriated by these days is anything to do with the 'over-sixties'. The over-sixties, to take a random selection, include

Mick Jagger, Charlotte Rampling, Janet Street-Porter, me – do you see any obvious similarity? Me neither. What politicians mean when they talk about 'the over-sixties' is people who are over sixty and vote entirely from financial self-interest – i.e. they vote for bus passes and winter-fuel allowance, and against, say, better schools or maternity services because they are too old to benefit. But of course the majority of over-sixties have children and grandchildren whom they might also be expected to care about. It is a mistake to picture them all as the sort of money-crazed Scrooges who care more about their bus passes than their grandchildren's schools. Sorry about that little rant. But the point I was trying to make is that interviews are valuable because they cut across the media tendency to lump us all into stereotypes.

I notice that women, more than men, are uncomfortable with difference and seem to want to assert similarity. 'Oh I'm just the same,' they cry delightedly as if they were playing Snap. Snap, I go to Cornwall for my holidays, snap, I have a wood-burning stove, snap, I prefer Nigella to Jamie. But how boring! Life would be intolerable if everyone were really just the same. I have friends who get agitated if I say I hate the theatre. They love the theatre, they feel obscurely threatened or undermined if I say I hate it, they want to convert me. But I'm not, absolutely *not*, trying to undermine them. I want *them* to enjoy the theatre, and even to tell me about it – I just don't want to go myself. That's fair enough, isn't it? I have one group of friends in the country who are mad keen on fox-hunting and a much larger group of friends in London who think it's barbaric. I probably think it's barbaric too (or I do, sitting here at my desk in London, watching the foxes stroll around my garden) but I love seeing my hunting friends in their kit and asking about their day afterwards, and admiring their impressive bruises. Also, in an overcrowded island it is important that different people like different things – if everyone wanted to spend their Saturdays in Westfield shopping mall, or everyone wanted to spend them visiting National Trust houses, there just wouldn't be room for us all.

Likewise, one must accept that other people have different ideas of what personal qualities are important. I was brought up to believe that intelligence was everything, that the world was basically divided between clever-clogs (like the Barbers) and thickos. I no longer believe that. I don't denigrate intelligence – it's a useful thing to have – but I now know it's not the be-all and end-all. Emotional intelligence is far more important. It's one of the first things I look for in interviewees, trying to assess whether they have any self-awareness and any awareness of me. I remember an interview with the late Lord Rees-Mogg where he told me at length 'what mothers want' without seemingly at any point wondering whether I might be a mother and might have some views on the subject. It was as if he was giving a lecture on Kalahari Bushmen to the National Geographic Society. There are plenty of men (invariably men) who talk in this way, as if addressing a public meeting. They don't seem to notice I am there, let alone ask themselves *why* I am there, and I often wonder if I could slip out and go to the loo and come back to find their peroration rolling on. Such people are quite fun to interview because you can suddenly prick their balloon with a rude question and watch them deflate. Sometimes I don't even ask a rude question, I ask a completely random question like: Were you breast-fed? just to bring them back to earth.

A category of people I admire but still find difficult to understand are the risk-takers, who tend to include most politicians, entrepreneurs and actors. Being very risk-averse myself, I used to assume that everyone *really* wanted security, and that they'd just been unlucky if they hadn't achieved it. But now I know that some people thrive on risk and get bored without it. As soon as they are comfortable in a job, or a house, or a marriage, they get itchy feet and head off to fresh fields and pastures new. Such people often achieve great things, and have adventurous lives – I envy them in some ways, but I could never emulate them because it would cause me too many sleepless nights.

Another way in which I differ from many (probably most) of my interviewees is that I am slow whereas they are fast. Some people simply have a lot more energy than others and can pack more into each day. I often ask my interviewees what they're doing for the rest of the week and feel positively faint when they tell me their schedule. I'm thinking I couldn't do all that in a month, never mind a week. I'm also amazed by the way artists like Tracey Emin or Sarah Lucas can seemingly produce work like an apple tree produces apples, without worrying about it. I wish I could be the same.

One real problem with interviewing is that it is hard to judge whether your subjects are self-centred. On the one hand, you want them to talk only about themselves, you encourage them to do that, and feel the time has been well spent if they do. But then it is difficult to identify whether they would *always* talk only about themselves, whether they are truly self-obsessed, or whether they are just being good, dutiful interviewees. So I usually try to put in one question like: Who helped you get started? or: What colleagues have been most valuable? to give them at least an opportunity of talking about, and hopefully praising, other people.

I like to ask about people's attitudes to money – whether they prefer spending on themselves or on others, whether they resent paying income tax, whether they remember their first pay cheque or wage packet – businessmen like Alan Sugar always can – and what was the first big purchase they ever made. I ask when they first paid out of their own pocket to fly business- or first-class – something I still haven't been able to bring myself to do. I ask women what's the most they've ever spent on a dress or handbag, and men what they've spent on a car.

A question I often ask is: Do you prefer being a guest or a host? Some people can hardly bear to be guests because it is so important to them to be in control. Being a guest means having to abide by someone else's tastes and preferences whereas being a host means you can make the rules. I doubt if Madonna often goes to stay with anyone. An alternative question is: Do you prefer giving presents or receiving them? Tracey Emin is wonderfully generous in giving presents but absolutely hopeless at receiving them. You are expected to give her *something* for her birthday, but then she often unwraps it and puts it down with no comment at all. After she'd done this for several years, I said, 'Look, Tracey, what *should* I give you for your birthdays because you never seem to like what I bring,' and she said, 'Oh no, oh no, I like everything you've given me.' It was tempting – but too cruel – to ask, 'So what do you remember that I've given you?' I once spent *hours* in a specialist doll's house shop, choosing a fabulously expensive antique miniature teapot because I knew she collected them, but she never said thank you. For her fiftieth, I gave her a pen.

Sense of humour is easy to assess: if someone tells you they have one then you can take it for granted that they don't. Or ask them to tell you a joke – that usually shuts them up. There are some questions that are not worth asking. If you ask someone if they're snobbish they will invariably say no. But if they volunteer, unasked, that they are not snobbish, you can take it that they are. Racist ditto, sexist ditto. Then there is the weird business of people who tell you that they love their children. I never ask if someone loves their children because I always assume that they do, but if they *tell* you they do, alarm bells start ringing.

When I started as an interviewer I was often told off for being 'too judgemental'. But surely you have to exercise judgement? We do it in real life after all – decide that we like so-and-so's new girlfriend on the basis of a very short meeting and without the real grilling that I would give her. Anyway I notice that readers are disappointed if I don't offer some hint of a verdict on whether I liked the person or not. Sometimes I simply can't because I'm unsure myself, but I always think of those as 'failed' interviews. I know it is unrealistic to believe that you can arrive at a judgement on someone on the basis of merely an hour or two's conversation but I am probably better at it than most, simply because I've been doing it so long. And most of my verdicts – though not all – have stood the test of time. Sometimes, years later, someone will come up to me at a party and say, 'You know, you were right about so and so. I worked with her for a year and she was a monster.' It's always funny when PRs do it. At the time, they utter indignant complaints about how you traduced their client, but once they're no longer working for her, they're happy to tell you all the horrible things she did.

I'm sounding smug now. Must stop. One of the many reasons I miss David was because he was very good at telling me when I sounded smug. Anyway, I've had a wonderful life being an interviewer. It's kept me entertained; I hope it's kept the readers entertained. And who would ever have thought that I could make such a long, curious career out of being nosy!

Acknowledgements

I should like to thank Georgia Garrett, my agent, and Alexandra Pringle and all the team at Bloomsbury for making this book happen. And a special thank-you to Della Fathers who encouraged me to keep going when I was inclined to give up.

I should also like to thank the many editors who enabled me to flourish as a journalist all these years – Ron Hall on the *Sunday Express*, Ian Jack on the *Independent on Sunday*, Graydon Carter on *Vanity Fair*, Roger Alton, John Mulholland, Nicola Jeal and Jane Ferguson on the *Observer*, and John Witherow, Martin Ivens and Sarah Baxter on the *Sunday Times*. But the one who taught me most was dear departed Harry Fieldhouse of *Penthouse*.